REAGAN SPEAKS

Reagan Speaks

THE MAKING OF AN AMERICAN MYTH

Paul D. Erickson

New York University Press
NEW YORK AND LONDON   1985

Quotations from the speeches contained herein were taken from the book, A TIME
FOR CHOOSING, published by Regnery Gateway, Inc., 940 North Shore Drive, Lake
Bluff, IL 60044.

Grateful acknowledgment is given to the *New York Times* for permission to reprint
copyrighted material. Copyright © 1980/84/85 by the New York Times Company.
Reprinted by permission.

Grateful acknowledgment is given to E. P. Dutton, Inc. for permission to quote excerpts
from WHERE'S THE REST OF ME? by Ronald Reagan and Richard G. Hubler.

Grateful acknowledgment is given to Sidgwick & Jackson Ltd. for permission to quote
excerpt from WHERE'S THE REST OF ME? by Ronald Reagan and Richard G.
Hubler.

Grateful acknowledgment is given to the Putnam Publishing Group and to Lou Cannon
for permission to quote excerpts from from REAGAN by Lou Cannon. Copyright
© 1982 by Lou Cannon.

Library of Congress Cataloging-in-Publication Data

Erickson, Paul D., 1954–
Reagan speaks.

Bibliography: p.
Includes index.
1. Reagan, Ronald—Oratory.   2. Political oratory—
United States.   3. United States—Politics and
government—1981–   I. Title.
E877.2.E64   1985   973.927'092'4   85-15277
ISBN 0–8147–2167–2

Designed by Ken Venezio

*I dedicate this book to my mother, Nancy,
with appreciation for her care,
and with admiration for her example.*

Can't we see that it is, after all, works of fiction, no matter how medi-ocre they may be artistically, that best arouse political passions?

—*Roland Barthes*

What Art really reveals to us is Nature's lack of design, her curious crudities, her extraordinary monotony, her absolutely unfinished con-dition. Nature has good intentions, but, as Aristotle once said, she cannot carry them out.

—*Oscar Wilde*

Rhetoric is the cemetery of human realities, or at any rate a home for the aged.

—*Jose Ortega y Gasset*

CONTENTS

PREFACE

Reagan Speaks: The Making of an American Myth examines
President Reagan's technique as a teller of tales who captured the
hearts and imaginations of a majority of the electorate in the first
half of the 1980s through the skillful use of what may be either
idealistic inspiration or cynical manipulation. Chapter One in-
troduces the major questions and approaches of the study. Chapter Two considers Reagan's development of a rhetorical style and
narrative persona, showing how he has throughout his acting and
political careers adopted a number of more or less imaginary
personalities. Chapter Three examines how Reagan moves back
and forth between the rhetorical world of his speeches and political realities, and how his techniques translate the audience into
characters in his fictive parables. Then in Chapter Four we will
look carefully at the stock characterizations which the President
employs to symbolize us and those whom he sees as our enemies.
Chapter Five places Reagan's story about Americans and their

foes in a wider context, specifically a battle between ultimate good and evil cast generally in the terms of Christian apocalypse and the jeremiad tradition. In Chapter Five we also note how Reagan presents matters of undeniably mundane import as sudden crises, thereby giving any issue he chooses the trappings of a tremendous emergency. The sixth chapter looks at the rhetoric of the 1984 presidential campaign, an oratorical event notable for many reasons, but perhaps most of all because in it we saw the Democrats and Republicans offering profoundly different visions of the American people and of their character. Chapter Seven comments on the state of political rhetoric today.

Throughout the text, I will use words such as *fictive, narrative,* and *mythic.* These terms all imply an artistic remove from cold facts, and that is all that I intend for them to signify. It is crucial at the outset to make unequivocally clear that this book is intended as neither a critique of the Reagan administration, nor as an encomium on the President. Readers seeking such treatments should look elsewhere. Striving for objectivity, I will deal as strictly as possible with the textual evidence of Ronald Reagan's ideas and feelings about the American people. I should perhaps warn the reader that an analysis of the sort that this book provides inevitably turns up flaws, inconsistencies, and glaring instances of presumption and manipulations of facts and things resembling facts. We will also discover a good deal of writing that some will judge trite, tasteless, and sentimental prose, as well as an abundance of tortured grammar, twisted syntax, and other stylistic atrocities. (Although the transcripts of President Reagan's speeches contain frequent errors in grammar and punctuation, and many inconsistencies in style, I have resisted my English teacher's impulse to repair the mistakes and have followed the original texts scrupulously throughout.) We will find splendid poetic passages as well, although less frequently. Final judgements of taste, however, as well as ultimate political evaluations, I leave to the reader. And with the reader they belong, for my task is the development of skills for understanding our President and our world. This book seeks to help to explain a remarkable phenomenon and to make us more careful listeners.

I should make my own biases clear. I have never voted for President Reagan, yet at the same time I sometimes find him a strikingly likeable person. On occasion, his speeches anger me, but at times I find myself inspired by Reagan's grand vision of this country. With the aid of several readers, Republicans and Democrats, I have sought to prevent my private politics from interfering with a study that I hope will interest readers without regard to ideology. Finally, I must confess that as a student of literature and language and not of political science or history, I have considerably less expertise in these latter areas than will many of my readers. I hope that readers who disagree with my interpretation of events will be patient.

This book has other important limits in that it does not pay much attention to genres of communication other than prepared remarks. Ideally, we should consider every aspect of political expression: commercials, signs, the ways in which candidates appear in photographs, and the other details labored over by consultants . Studies of those subjects exist, and I refer the reader to my bibliography for places to learn about the packaging of candidates. As the formal utterances of the President, Reagan's orations stand as the clearest expression we have of what he believes and preaches to us and of what a majority of American voters responded to positively from 1980 until at least 1984. Reagan's speeches are artifacts of his public persona, as well as manifestations of the dreams and concerns that Americans felt most deeply in his time. As this book goes to press, Reagan has reorganized his White House staff—a move which many expect will have a strong impact on his speeches. It remains to be seen if the rhetoric of President Reagan's second term will differ substantially from that of his previous career, and I look forward to analyses of the speeches written under Donald Regan and Patrick Buchanan with great interest.

ACKNOWLEDGMENTS

Writing this book has given me an excuse and the time to think long and hard about President Reagan, and to ponder what his rhetoric suggests about our national psyche in the 1980s. The project has also prompted innumerable fascinating conversations. Writing a book gives one license to pester all sorts of people with questions. As a student of literature rather than of political science, I am especially grateful to those who patiently shared their expertise and wisdom with me.

My greatest thanks go to George Jepsen, who first suggested the undertaking, and who has in the years of our friendship generously shared his insights into politics. George's dedication to public service and to the continuing success of democratic government are a constant inspiration.

Mentors, advisers, colleagues, and friends have been invaluable. Chief among these are Richard Neustadt and David Gergen, who very early explained to me the process of writing presidential

Acknowledgments

addresses. Molly Tuthill of the Hoover Institute was most helpful. Sacvan Bercovitch, Daniel Aaron, Joel Porte, James Engell, and W. J. Bate, all of the Harvard University Department of English and American Literature and Language, deserve special thanks. Tony Downer, Eliot Cohen, Robert Distel, Betsy Lehman, Joseph Cooper, James Dowaliby, Rita Jepsen, Barbara Earle, David Stanford, Keith Varner, Elisabeth and Roger Swain, Joel Dando, Mark Parker, Kevin Van Anglen, Peter Clark, Richard Grossman, and Sue Watts earned my gratitude by answering questions, sharing thoughts, and offering encouragement. David and Mimi Aloian and the students and Senior Common Room of Quincy House listened to parts of this book in early versions, and so gave me important chances to test and to develop my ideas. I am indebted to Master Aloian as well for making available to me the *sine qua non* of scholarship—a quiet place to write. Harvard's Committee on History and Literature also quite graciously allowed me to speak on my work. Undertaking a cross-disciplinary study, I very much appreciated the intellectual companionship of the faculty and students whom I met in History and Literature.

Kitty Moore, Despina Papazoglou, Colin Jones, and Robert L. Bull, III have strengthened the book and made my first experience in publishing a joy.

Finally, I thank my old friend Tim Bent and my wife Chenoweth Moffatt, both of whom not only gave me enormous moral support while tolerating my frenzies of work, but who also read and improved the entire manuscript in its several stages.

Many others deserve mention, and I apologize for any omissions. My thanks to you, named and unnamed; I hope that you above all will find the enterprise worthwhile.

Quincy House
April 30, 1985

REAGAN SPEAKS

1 / INTRODUCTION

Ronald Reagan is by far the most persuasive political speaker of our time. He derives remarkable power from his use of language. Even his opponents grant him the title Great Communicator. To better understand how Reagan's rhetoric functions, though, we should remember that the word *communication* means more than clear speaking or writing. It comes from the Latin *communico*, which includes in its meanings "to share" and "to unite, to join together." Clearer echoes of these sometimes forgotten meanings survive in *community,* and in *communion*—a word that in religion denotes joining in worship as a body of *communicants* under the spiritual leadership of a preacher. Communication in this sense is not simply the transfer of information from one person to another but a unifying process of commitment to the values and beliefs presented by the communicator. Just as a minister tells his congregation what to believe about the cosmos, so does Ronald Reagan analogously preach to America his own political gospel. And like the priest who must, above all, instill faith in the hearts of his flock, so does President Reagan seek to inspire us.

The overarching theme of Reagan's rhetoric has been a restoration of our communal beliefs. "One of my dreams," he told the American Bar Association in 1983 in a typical expression, "is to help Americans rise above pessimism by renewing their belief in themselves."[1] The word *belief* has several implications here. It means a restoration of national self-confidence in domestic and foreign affairs. It also refers to having faith in the American Dream, that curious and variously defined myth of America that holds that we are a chosen people, blessed by God and acting as his agents on this earth. This vision of America has roots deep in our history, reaching back to the earliest days of European settlement. The Puritans came to New England with a vision of the New World as the future kingdom of Christ on Earth. "The Lord will be our God," John Winthrop told a band of settlers in a sermon quoted frequently by Reagan,

and delight to dwell among us as his own people, and will command a blessing upon us in all our ways, so that we shall see much more of his wisdom, power, goodness, and truth, than formerly we have been acquainted with.[2]

The Puritans of Massachusetts fused their Christianity with civic doctrine. Dissenters from the faith found little welcome in the body politic. Their theocratic spirit persisted beyond the end of Puritan theological hegemony as their descendants shared with new immigrants a general sense that America was a promised land set apart for various reasons by God for this new chosen people. Even when the overtly Christian overtones faded, the notion of America as the New Israel of economic, political, or moral blessing survived. Successive visions have dominated the American Dream, changing with circumstances and appearing in forms as diverse as radical democracy, manifest destiny, and a belief that we are the "last best hope of man on earth," to use a line of Abraham Lincoln's that Reagan often quotes. The many different creeds and interpretations of the American Dream are the several denominations of the American civil religion, that at times confused but nevertheless potent set of convictions and visions that translates history into mythology and life into a dream.

Civil religion shares many of the characteristics of church religion. The Washington Monument, Lincoln Memorial, and Monticello are shrines and temples that draw worshipers who *believe in* our government both by agreeing with its principles philosophically and by showing their devotion to it in more emotional and quasi-religious ways. The Father of Our Country, Honest Abe, Old Hickory, Camelot's John Kennedy, and other fictionalized leaders are our saints, and we recall them especially on our Holy days: Independence, Thanksgiving, and Memorial days, for example.[3] And we have our priests and prophets, among whom the president is usually considered the most important.

To a large extent the romanticization of our history is an unconscious phenomenon. Obeying some mysterious impulse— one akin, perhaps, to those which moved earlier societies to turn history into folklore and then into mythological religions—we transform our human leaders into demigods. George Washington, whose eulogists compared him to Moses, Joshua, and even to Christ, was changed from an exceptionally able administrator into the quasi-divine Father of Our Country. This fictive deification has a constant subliminal effect on how we perceive the nation and its presidency. The chief executive somehow rises above mortality into a state of superhumanity. We must, we are told from childhood on, always respect the president, simply because he *is* the president, the direct and democratically annointed heir of Washington. Every president since the first has found himself defined in important ways by the popular notion of his symbolic role.[4]

The institution of the presidency limits and controls what an individual president can do. This is true not only in that the Constitution restricts the legal authority of the office, and in the fact that various bureaucratic establishments hinder initiatives, but also in terms of the symbolic acts and utterances of the president. But at the same time that the traditions of our civil religion manipulate each president, so do they give him enormous power. Speaking from the nation's loftiest podium-pulpit, the president has at his disposal a powerful array of symbolic tools. No one speaks to or for the nation more significantly than a popular president. Embodying our projected national hopes and beliefs, our presidents serve as the makers and manipulators—as well as the inheritors and servants—of the icons of the myth of America. By acting as the priests of this purportedly blessed land, our leaders use symbolic language charged with the tenets of our civic faith to persuade us and to bring us into communion with their particular vision and policies. The success of a president depends in large measure on his ability to solve economic and foreign affairs problems, but even more on his talent for communicating with the electorate. In other words, it is determined by how effectively he can persuade us *to believe* through the use of symbolic actions and language as well as through genuine administrative accomplishments.

Politicians have at their disposal a wide range of rhetorical devices that can connect them to one degree or another with what the voting public might consider "the soul of America." One such method is simply to invoke the saints of the past, to claim direct ideological and spiritual descent from various Founding Fathers and intermediaries—be they Washington and Jefferson, Lincoln, Franklin Roosevelt, or, as is the case more often than not today, John F. Kennedy. Reagan does this, but much more interesting and powerful are the more subtle ways in which he creates a gospel of America. As we will see, Reagan derives his most potent rhetorical symbols from the apparently less exalted sources of our daily lives, from our contemporary folklore in forms as diverse as movies, television, and the like.

The claims of Lincoln, Wilson, and both Roosevelts notwithstanding, Reagan is in at least one sense our most literary president.[5] Others have used more poetically splendid tropes, and we will probably never see Reagan's speeches in anthologies of American literature (as we do those of Lincoln and Franklin Roosevelt). Not a man of letters by the refined aesthetic standards of belles-lettres, Reagan is still supremely literary by virtue of the methods which he employs in his rhetoric. I do not refer to the technical devices of classical oratory—zeugma, apostrophe, and chiasmus, for example—but to the simple fact that Ronald Reagan tells stories to make his points.[6] He speaks, as it were, in parables, and his overall rhetoric of the American Dream is itself a grand parable that translates history into an epic of mythological proportions. This constant transformation of political material into stories is, in fact, the chief distinction of Reagan's rhetoric.

Reagan told a typical story to a California audience as they bid him farewell in his January, 1981 trip to the White House inaugural. He spoke about the work before him, of the hopes and dreams that he sought to make real, and of the nation whose leader he would soon become. He told the audience a tale of two awards for bravery: the United States' Congressional Medal of Honor, and the Soviet Union's equivalent decoration. One of the President's most frequently used examples, this is a concise and stirring expression of his vision of the two countries. Reagan came upon the first part of the tale while working as an adjutant in the Army during World War II.

A B-17 coming back across the channel from a raid over Europe, badly shot up by antiaircraft, the ball turret that hung underneath the belly of the plane had taken a hit. The young ball-turret gunner was wounded, and they couldn't get him out of the turret there while flying.

But over the channel, the plane began to lose altitude, and the commander had to order bail out. And as the men started to leave the plane, the last one to leave—the boy, understandably, knowing he was left behind to go down with the plane, cried out in terror—the last man to leave the plane saw the commander sit down on the floor. He took the boy's hand and said, "Never mind, son, we'll ride it down together." Congressional Medal of Honor, posthumously awarded.

Reagan found the second part of his story, that of the Soviet hero, years later when he read that the Soviet Union had awarded its highest award to a man without saying exactly why. Curious, he looked into the matter with the aid of a journalist. He discovered that the Soviet hero was a Spaniard who had worked as a translator during the Spanish Civil War, and then lived in Moscow, Mexico, and Cuba. He had spent 23 years in a Mexican jail, and Mr. Reagan found the matter altogether perplexing. Finally, though, the truth came out, as he explained: "He was the man who buried that ice axe mountaineers [*sic*], mountain climbers carry in the head of Leon Trotsky."[7]

The two-part story of heroes and their societies serves as a powerful allegory for Reagan's concept of America and her chief antagonist: "They in another society give their highest honor to a political assassin. We gave ours to a man who would sacrifice his life simply to bring comfort to a boy who had to die," said, Reagan; "I think that explains the great difference between our societies. . . . The bedrock of our strength is America's moral and spiritual character."

We see in President Reagan's short parable all the standard elements of fiction: characters (those in the vignettes and the nations which they represent), settings (the plane and the scene of Trotsky's death), plot (what happened in the stories as well as how the two governments responded), theme (the contrast between America and the Soviet Union), and narrative point of view (Reagan's politics). The allegory works on three levels: as a stirring tale of American patriotism and kindness and of Soviet degradation; as an expression of Reagan's ideology; and as a vehicle for the President as narrator to make himself part of a potent story. The episodes of the medals are really subplots in the tale of Ronald Reagan, the man who discovered something profound in contemplating the two awards. The most important story is that which the teller enacts in the telling. He recounts for us two tales, and then, by depicting his own reaction, gives an example of how to respond to them in ideological and emotional terms. This is much more than an account of two honors. It is a psychodrama starring President Reagan and bringing his listeners into communion with his experience of interpreting the original texts. The matter becomes all the more striking when we realize that after reporters called the truth of the story about the American airmen into question, Reagan dropped it from his repertoire.[8]

One effect of the Reagan revolution has been an increased desire for powerful speakers. Mario Cuomo, Gary Hart, Jesse Jackson, and Edward Kennedy have all recently received attention from liberals for their speaking abilities; on the right, conservatives wonder how their party will fair when the Great Communicator no longer speaks for them. Senator Robert Dole's ability to appeal to the Senate (and to national television audiences) was reportedly a factor in his election to Senate majority leader.

Yet political oratory should be considered suspect. Perhaps Daniel Boorstin's advice is more necessary today than it was twenty years ago. "Nowadays everybody tells us that what we need is more belief, a stronger and deeper and more encompassing faith," wrote Boorstin in words that foreshadowed Reagan's insistence on a revival of belief in America,

. . . faith in America and in what we are doing. That may be true in the long run. What we need first and now is to disillusion ourselves. What ails us most is not what we have substituted for America. We suffer primarily not from our vices or our weaknesses, but from our illusions. We are haunted, not by reality, but by those images we have put in place of reality.[9]

We need to remember the differences between facts and fiction, between history and myth, and between hopes and realistic expectations. Recognizing the devices of rhetoric and learning how to see through them will, as Boorstin put it so well, help us to "clear away the fog so we can face the world we share with all mankind." If after finishing this book, the reader becomes more aware of how Reagan and others (all along the political spectrum) use language as a weapon in their battles, then the time spent in its composition will have been well-used. Perhaps we can best describe *Reagan Speaks* as a book literary of criticism for politicians and voters, an extension of analytic methods from the classroom and scholarly journal to the electoral arena.

We should keep in mind that Reagan devotes a good deal of energy to his speeches, but that he rarely if ever writes them himself. When he arrived at the White House the new President delivered a packet of old speeches to his new speechwriting office with instructions that they learn to imitate his style and substance. Reagan has a large and diverse staff of researchers and speechwriters who prepare the texts for most of his addresses; other speeches originate from various departments of the executive branch—from the State Department, for example, when the President speaks to foreign parliaments or to the United Nations.[10]

Does it matter for us that Reagan does not write his own material? Not a great deal. While that fact should affect how we evaluate Reagan as an individual—including his fitness for office—it need not interfere with our present study of how his words operate on us. When we read or watch *King Lear,* the question of whether or not William Shakespeare actually wrote the play is inconsequential outside of scholarly circles. We respond to the spectacle of Lear's folly and of his daughters' treachery without regard to questions of authorship. When Lear's daughters banish him to the heath and Gloucester's eyes are plucked from their sockets, our pity and horror hardly depend on quarrels fought in scholarly journals over attribution.

Similarly, when we hear our President speak to us, the words and messages affect us as if they were purely his, no matter who

8

might have chosen, arranged, and edited them. Nearly every major politician employs ghost-writers. Although this practice adds to the confusing subterfuges by which public figures might delude the electorate, we accept it as a necessary expedient in campaigning and governing. Almost no officials have the time or the talent to write their own material.

To dismiss Reagan's rhetoric as artistically impure would be to apply largely unrealistic and irrelevant standards. Voters simply do not respond to their president strictly as an individual, but as something of an institution. Ronald Reagan may bring many of his own ideas and convictions to his office, but beyond any doubt he is the spokesman for the batteries of hired advisors, counselors, and for his constituency at large. We do not separate Ronald Reagan the individual from Ronald Reagan as a political symbol when we respond to him in his presidential capacity. This is not as things should be, but nevertheless the attitude pervades our image of him.

It makes no difference in this regard who writes the words pronounced by President Reagan. The object of our scrutiny, and of our votes, is not Ronald Reagan the man, but the Great Communicator who stands at the head of the nation, and who speaks to us as a people more powerfully and persuasively than any president has since Franklin Delano Roosevelt. By scrutinizing the ways in which he portrays the United States, our citizens, our enemies and allies, and himself as our leader, we should discover much about Ronald Reagan and, along the way, about ourselves. Our symbols speak not only to us and for us, but also about us.

NOTES

1. Unless otherwise indicated, all quotations from Reagan speeches dating before January, 1981, come from Alfred Balitzer, editor, A *Time for Choosing: The Speeches of Ronald Reagan, 1961–1982* (Chicago: Regnery Gateway Press, 1983). Speeches by Reagan after January 20, 1981 are from *The*

Weekly Compilation of Presidential Documents (Washington, D.C.: Office of the Federal Register, National Archives and Records Service, General Services Administration).

2. John Winthrop, "A Model of Christian Charity," in Alan Heimert and Andrew Delbanco, editors, *The Puritans in America: A Narrative Anthology* (Cambridge: Harvard University Press, 1985), pp. 81–92.

3. For a number of insightful essays on American civil religion see Donald G. Jones and Russell E. Richey, editors, *American Civil Religion* (New York: Harper and Row, 1974).

4. Jimmy Carter's deliberate demystification of himself (as exemplified by his walking the inaugural parade route in 1977 and by the other overtly "human" aspects of his projected persona) was an attempt to undo nearly two centuries of myth making. Of course, this very quality of Carter's administration has been blamed for his failure to stay in power. We clearly prefer our presidents to have a grander stature than Mr. Carter thought they should have. See Jimmy Carter, *Keeping Faith* (New York: Bantam Books, 1982), and John H. Patton, "A Government as Good as its People: Jimmy Carter and the Restoration of Transcendence to Politics," *Quarterly Journal of Speech*, 63 (October, 1977), pp. 249–57; and Dan F. Hahn, "The Rhetoric of Jimmy Carter, 1976–1980," *Presidential Studies Quarterly*, XIV, 2 (1984), pp. 289–315.

5. Most writers on political oratory rank the speeches of Lincoln, Wilson, and Franklin Roosevelt as stylistic highpoints. Some include Thomas Jefferson and Theodore Roosevelt in a list of literary presidents, not so much for their speeches, but by virtue of their other writings.

6. For a good textbook on classical rhetoric, see Edward P. J. Corbett, *Classical Rhetoric for the Modern Student* (New York: Oxford University Press, 1971).

7. No verbatim record of the Los Angeles speech exists. Since Reagan has told the story with little variation, I feel confident in using the text of Reagan's "Congressional Medal of Honor Society" speech (Dec. 12, 1983) *The Weekly Compilation of Presidential Documents* (Washington, D.C.: Office of the Federal Register, National Archives and Records Service, General Services Administration, 1983).

8. *The New York Times*, September 20, 1984, p. B-12.

9. Daniel Boorstin, *The Image: Or What Happened to the American Dream* (New York: Atheneum, 1962), p. 6.

10. This was explained to me by David Gergen, former Director of Communications for the Reagan White House, in a conversation in the spring of 1984. Ghost-writing is not a recent development. The first reported practitioners of formal rhetoric were Corax and Tisias of Syracuse, who wrote speeches for an early Greek democracy in the fifth century, B.C. Plato banned poets from his Republic because he feared their irrational unreliability; less well-known is his exclusion of professional speakers and ghost-

writers, whom he distrusted morally as well as psychologically. William Pitt, Patrick Henry, George Washington, Daniel Webster, Winston Churchill, and John Kennedy all relied on speechwriters to some extent. Franklin Roosevelt institutionalized an informal White House speechwriting staff, the form of which continued through the Truman, Kennedy, and Johnson administrations. Used to a team of aides, Eisenhower had a formal office to write his speeches. Nixon, Ford, and Carter followed this arrangement. Reagan wrote his own speeches until the midsixties; when he arrived at the White House he delivered a stack of old texts to his new staff for stylistic study. Under Reagan, the speechwriting operation in the White House has grown quite sophisticated and involves a large body of creative and policy experts. I had hoped to visit the Reagan speechwriting office, and I spoke with someone there throughout the summer of 1984. An interview seemed in the offing, but for whatever reasons—perhaps the pressures of the campaign—the office stopped returning my calls.

2 / A TIME FOR CHOOSING

Ronald Reagan launched his political career with a single speech delivered 16 years before his election to the presidency. On October 27, 1964, as Barry Goldwater headed for almost total electoral defeat by Lyndon Johnson, Reagan appeared on national television to deliver "A Time for Choosing"—better known as "The Speech." When first encouraged by California Republicans to make Reagan's speech part of his own national appeal, Goldwater's advisors rejected it as far too reactionary even for the message of their campaign. They feared that Reagan's promised attack on the most basic tenets of American liberalism and the New Deal would alienate all but the most right-wing element of Goldwater's supporters. They proposed instead to rebroadcast a program entitled "Brunch with Barry," which featured the Senator mildly explaining his ideas to a group of housewives. Goldwater intervened, though, and "The Speech" ran on national television.

Ronald Reagan spent decades preparing for his national political debut. His experience as an orator dates back to 1928, when, as a freshman at Eureka College, the future chief executive led a student strike against a school president who wanted to cut special programs and to reduce his teaching staff in order to save money. When Reagan spoke to his classmates and teachers at a heated meeting, they rose to their feet with acclamation. The strikers won. Eureka's budget-minded president resigned and Ronald Reagan went on to become head of the student government. Recalling the prophetic meeting, he has written, "I discovered that night that an audience has a feel to it and, in the parlance of the theater, that audience and I were together."[1] The incident strikes us for two reasons. First, we note the amusingly ironic fact that the man who would one day arrest student demonstrators and later call for budget reductions in education began his career by attacking a university president whose policies one might compare to what Reagan himself would espouse in the future.

The second, and much more significant aspect of the incident, is Reagan's description of it in theatrical terms. Recalling his very first political utterance, Reagan characterized his listeners as an audience and himself as an actor who used words not just to convey ideas but to achieve a subliminal identification. Kenneth Burke, one of this century's most insightful scholars concerning the use of rhetoric, sees political address and dramatic acting as two forms of the same thing. In both cases, argued Burke, speakers aim for what he calls *consubstantiation*, a super-identification of the audience with the actor/orator in which listeners suspend their sense of individuality and see the speaker as a projection of themselves as a group. In speaking and in listening, both parties make an imaginative leap into a common persona. We might be tempted to dismiss Reagan's comment as superficial;

on the contrary, it illustrates his perhaps unconcious recognition of an important principle of political communication: the rhetorical experience of uniting an audience in the words and character of one seeking to persuade them.

Reagan's voice and ability to use language to establish this emotional link with listeners lies behind every success he has ever attained. As Roger Rosenblatt wrote in *Time*, Reagan's voice: ". . . recedes at the right moments, turning mellow at points of intensity. When it wishes to be most persuasive, it hovers barely above a whisper so as to win you over by intimacy, if not by substance. . . . He likes his voice, treats it like a guest. He makes you part of the hospitality. It was that voice that carried him out of Dixon and away from the Depression . . ."[2] As a child, Reagan won praise and approval by appearing in community plays staged by his mother, and he acted throughout high school and college. After graduating from Eureka, Reagan put his voice to work in radio.

Along with the mastery of his voice modulation, Reagan early on had a remarkable talent for creating and telling stories. Lou Cannon reports one of Reagan's favorite memories from his time as a sports announcer for WHO. A small station with limited resources, WHO relied on the inventiveness of its announcer to make up for their lack of live on-the-scene reporting. Reagan sat in a booth and, using sketchy wire-service bulletins, pretended that he was broadcasting directly from the stadium. He had a phenomenal ability to create verbal illusions: "You just couldn't believe that you were not actually there," recalls WHO's program director.[3] On at least one occasion, Reagan was even more inventive. He once found himself in the middle of a pitch with nothing to work from in the way of a script:

When the slip came through [from the person in charge of the wire-service machine], it said, "The wire's gone dead." Well, I had the ball on the way to the plate. And I figured real quick, I could say we'll tell them what happened and then play transcribed music, but in those days there were at least seven or eight other fellows that were doing the same game. I didn't want to lose the audience. So I thought real quick, "there's one thing that doesn't get in the scorebook," so I had Billy [Jurges] foul one off . . . and I had him foul one back at third base and described the fight between the two kids that were trying to get the ball. Then I had him foul one that just missed being a home run, about a foot and a half. And I did set a world record for successive fouls, or for someone standing there, except that no one keeps records of that kind. I was beginning to sweat when Curley [the monitor in the control booth] sat up straight and started typing . . . and the slip came through the window and I could hardly talk for laughing because it said, "Jurges popped out on the first ball pitched."[4]

Reagan tells the story recounted above as a charming and mildly self deprecating joke, but it shows us just how comfortable he can be with illusion. Having taken himself and his listeners into an imaginative stadium, the future President instantly turned to outright fiction to avoid losing his audience. Unwilling to break the spell by which he held them, Reagan simply lied, albeit harmlessly and for a motive which no one could hold against him.

Working from wire-service notes and his own imagination trained Reagan well for acting in movies. After exaggerating (and misrepresenting) his acting experience to a casting agent-whom he visited while covering the Chicago Cubs training camp, Reagan found himself in 1937 the newest member of the Warner Brothers studio.[5] Most of his roles hardly called for subtle acting talents. More often than not he appeared in entertaining and sentimental movies as a good-looking, earnest young man. Reagan describes himself as "the Erroll Flynn of the B's." Nevertheless, his talent for substituting fiction for fact and an adopted persona for his own brought him long way from Dixon, Illinois.

Yet, the successful actor eventually began to feel that the real Ronald Reagan was being overwhelmed by the illusions he was living. "I had become a semi-automaton 'creating' a character another had written, doing what still another person told me to do on the set," he wrote in his autobiography, *Where's the Rest of Me?*; "Seeing the rushes, I could barely believe the colored shadow on the screen was myself."[6] Reagan seems to have feared psychic annihilation, a common and deep-rooted concern for actors. Recalling how "in some weird way" he slipped into his character for *King's Row*—which he considers the high point of his acting career—Reagan has written of the seductive dangers of self-delusion: "So much of our profession is taken up with pretending, with the interpretation of never-never roles, that an actor must spend at least half his waking hours in fantasy, in rehearsal or shooting. If he is only an actor, I feel, he is much like I was in *King's Row*, only half a man—no matter how great his talents."[7]

Despite these misgivings, Reagan did not reject acting outright. What he really wanted was not to rid himself of his imaginative impulse, but to put it to work on behalf of the right purpose. Notice that Reagan objected not to being an actor altogether, but to being *only* an actor. One could interpret this as an insistence that one devote time to a presumably more socially responsible endeavor. But Reagan's description of how discovering politics affected him supports the suggestion that what he sought was not two distinct and complementary sides to his life and psyche, but one personality that fused reality with imagination. "[W]hen I walked into the boardroom [of the Screen Actors Guild in 1938 to begin his adult political career], . . . I was beginning to find the *rest of* [i.e., not *another*] me"[8] Reagan disliked becoming a colored shadow because that meant "'creating' a character another had written, doing what still another person told me to do on the set." In moving from the movie screen to the boardroom and podium, Ronald Reagan could in effect become his own author and director. The impulse toward creating a character remained, but came under his own control.

As his description of the Eureka debut makes clear, entering politics did not mean giving up acting in any sense of the word.

In fact, Reagan's descriptions of his early union days suggest that at least on one level he saw politics as an experience similar to acting in films. Recalling the tumultuous days in which his guild struggled with purportedly Stalinist groups for control of Tinseltown, Reagan told an audience in 1961, "We lived through scenes that heretofore had been only make-believe." Art became life as the colored shadow stepped from the screen and into the world of politics and ideology. To say this is to assert nothing extraordinary about Ronald Reagan. As Oscar Wilde wrote, we all seek in our imaginings a more satisfying reality. Although more developed and exercised on a far grander scale than usual, Reagan's fictive impulse is quite normal.

Impressed by the acumen with which Reagan steered the movie-actors' union through this period of turmoil, the Screen Actors Guild elected him to the first of the six terms he would serve as its president. Reagan was an ardent Roosevelt Democrat in those days, but his liberalism only took him so far to the left. He did join two purported communist front organizations (the American Veterans Committee and the Hollywood Independent Citizens Committee of the Arts, Sciences, and Professions), then quit when he decided that they were dominated by Stalinists. By 1947, Reagan thoroughly believed a conspiracy existed to infiltrate the film industry and to exploit it to shape the ideas and emotions of American audiences and voters. Film, he realized, can exert great power as symbol and propaganda. Portraying bankers and industrialists as greedy scoundrels is a less-than-subtle example of how movies subliminally turn audiences away from capitalism. Less clumsy devices also exist in the myriad nuances that a director has at his or her disposal. Reagan was gaining a sound recognition of the political application of fiction—a wisdom with obvious implications for our understanding of his own persuasive methods.

Despite his fear of communism, Reagan approached the Hollywood furor with a tolerance unusual in that time. When testifying before the House Un-American Activities Committee, he refused to brand all labor organizers in Hollywood as communists, even taking the potentially dangerous step at that time of criticizing the sometimes overzealous spirit of the hearings:

> I detest, I abhor their philosophy, but I detest more than that their tactics, which are those of a fifth column, and are dishonest, but at the same time I never as a citizen want to see our country become urged, by either fear or resentment of this group, that we ever compromise with any of our democratic principles through that fear or resentment. I still think that democracy can do it.[9]

Compared to actors such as Gary Cooper, who admitted total ignorance of Marxist doctrine but called for the total banning of the Communist party, Ronald Reagan spoke quite fairly—even courageously, given the tenor of the times.

Life changed for Reagan in the late forties. His first wife, Jane Wyman, claimed that his growing obsession with politics bored her and she divorced him. At the same time his career as an actor went into a slump. Marriage to Nancy Davis (whom he met by clearing her of charges that she had been involved with communists) and the arrival of their first child put new financial pressures on Reagan. He looked for ways to rejuvenate his career. For two weeks he worked as a master of ceremonies in Las Vegas. Reagan made a hit in the clubs, but he found this work so distasteful that he quickly gave it up. With time on his hands, he turned to his second love, politics, becoming once again president of the Screen Actors Guild.

During his presidency of the union, Reagan earned a strong reputation as a political speaker (in part by arguing that actors deserved depreciation allowances on their taxes because their earning power would decrease inevitably as they aged and wrinkled). Well-known and popular, he received in 1954 an offer to act as the principle spokesman for the General Electric Corporation. His duties included hosting and occasionally starring in weekly episodes of *GE Theater*, and acting as the company's chief public relations agent. This new job exemplifies again how acting and giving speeches were commingled by Reagan to further his political career. Traveling around the country by train for eight years, Reagan spent over 4000 hours before company and civic groups, an experience that he says awoke him from the dreams of Hollywood: "When I went on those tours and shook hands with all those people," he told an interviewer in 1981, "I began to see that they were very different people than the people Hollywood was talking about. I was seeing the same people that I grew up with in Dixon, Illinois. I realized that I was living in a tinsel factory. And this exposure brought me back."[10] If we consider how closely Reagan associated acting with political speechmaking, we might well suspect this return to reality as yet another way in which he traded his Hollywood audience and persona for new ones.

At first Reagan carefully avoided relying on a single script. His early assignments were designed to boost morale within the company, and he spent the bulk of his time in G.E. factories, smiling and signing autographs for employees who wanted to shake hands with a movie and television star. Diverse company audiences called for different rhetorical approaches: speaking to clerical staff, assembly line workers, and scientific researchers meant that Reagan had to vary his talks constantly. "I knew I had to avoid a set routine or a canned speech, which, although it would have been easier, could have ruined the whole wonderful reaction we were getting," he wrote of the first trips.[11] In order to be "together" with the audience with which he was communicating, Reagan had to choose his subjects and words carefully; ad-libbing seemed by far the best approach, although for a trained actor or rhetor even ad-libbing draws on well-practiced words and gestures.

The situation changed within two years when General Electric decided to expand Reagan's duties to include public relations outside the firm. Reagan recalls an appearance in Boston as a turning point. It centered around a plan to collect money for charities and required a speech that would appeal to people from many backgrounds and interests. The event went well, and from then on Reagan's talks for General Electric became more and more thematically substantive. He replaced his brief words to star-struck workers with long and carefully composed speeches. Reagan wrote his own material at this time and gradually transformed his public appearances into the beginnings of something that resembled a political campaign. At the same time, Reagan started to put together his populist gospel:

I couldn't be a mouthpiece for someone else's thoughts. Like in those days right after the war, and later on when I took to the road in behalf of the motion picture industry, speaking wasn't a gimmick to justify a personal appearance. I had to have something I wanted to say, and something in which I believed.[12]

The rhetorical occasion came before the argument. Expected to have something to say, Reagan had to find a message and a text, "something [he] wanted to say." Choosing one, he remained constantly aware of the interests of his employers and of his audiences. For decades Reagan had worked from scripts, uttering the words of others; in spite of his fears of losing control and becoming "a colored shadow," he continued to act in this capacity as the corporate spokesman. His protestations of independence notwithstanding, Reagan mixed his own convictions with the ideals of his listeners and employer. He stayed "together" even with the new groups to whom he spoke.

As the years went on, my speeches underwent a kind of evolution, reflecting not only my changing philosophy but also the swiftly rising tide of collectivism that threatens to inundate what remains of our free economy. . . . I went out of my way to point out that the problems of centralizing power in Washington, with subsequent loss of freedom at the local level, were problems that crossed party lines. . . . [A] change . . . was taking place all over America. People wanted to talk about and hear about encroaching government control, and hopefully they wanted suggestions as to what they themselves could do to turn the tide.[13]

Reagan was happy to tell people what they wanted to hear. One biographer argues that Reagan's shift to the right was at least in part a desire to be "together" with the more conservative audiences whom he addressed at this time: "Reagan believes in what he says, and he wound up believing what he was saying."[14]

Reagan began to use a more or less fixed text with two themes: communist plots and the growing dangers posed by big government in America. Reagan arrived at these topics by way of his defense of the Hollywood community. In its earliest form "The Speech" consisted of a vindication of the film industry from what he considered sensationalist press attacks. To clear the majority of actors from suspicions cast during the congressional anticommunist hearings, Reagan put the blame where he felt it belonged by making "the most dramatic part of [his] pitch . . . the account of the attempted takeover of the industry by the communists."[15] This anti-Stalinist pitch turned into an assault on liberalism in America, which Reagan saw as the first step toward communist totalitarianism.

Rejecting his past as a confirmed Roosevelt Democrat, Reagan decried a range of New Deal institutions, most notably the Tennessee Valley Authority electric project. His comments raised the hackles of his corporate employers, though, who had a $50 million a year contract with the TVA. Reagan heard of the company's distress over his remarks, so he called up Chairman of the Board Ralph Cordiner. Lou Cannon reports Reagan's account of the conversation:

"Mr. Cordiner, I understand that you have a problem that has to do with me," Reagan said.

"Well, I'm sorry you found that out," Cordiner replied. "It's my problem. I've told them that we don't tell an employee what he can say or can't say, and we're not going to start."[16]

But Cordiner did admit that his life would be much easier if Reagan would decide to change his speech, and Reagan did so at once. "The responsibility was mine," he wrote; "How free was I to embarrass or hurt the company, just because I had carte blanche to speak my mind?" Reagan's most loyal biographers describe this episode as an example of how conservative businessmen like Ralph Cordiner will sell out their beliefs for the sake of a dollar. In fact, the incident argues exactly the opposite. Cordiner refused to force an employee to deny his convictions. Even though Reagan referred to the matter as an "attempted hatchet job," it was he—and not General Electric who did the censoring.[17]

A typical example of Reagan's speeches for General Electric was entitled "Encroaching Control: The Peril of Ever Expanding Government," which he delivered to the Phoenix Chamber of Commerce in March, 1961. "It must seem presumptuous to some of you for a member of my profession to stand here and attempt to talk on problems of the nation," he began. Hollywood was far removed from the lives of most Americans—or so it might have seemed. Recalling the strikes of the late forties, Reagan pointed to the film industry as a microcosm of what the entire nation was facing in the cold war years. "Ugly reality," he announced, "came to our town on direct orders of the Kremlin." Only by dint of courage and persistence did Reagan and his fellow actors drive communism out of their industry. But the onslaught had not really ended. "We now know of course that we only won an isolated battle," he continued; "They are crawling out from under the rocks; and memories being as short as they are, there are plenty of well-meaning but misguided people willing to give them a hand." Reagan claimed that his firsthand experience with communist infiltration qualified him for the task of warning America about the continuing menace. The way that he described the Stalinist campaign suggests that he considered his talent for communication an equally important asset. Reagan spoke of the propaganda aspects of the battle:

Most people agree that the ideological struggle with Russia is the number one problem in the world. Millions of words are used almost daily to record the fluctuating temperature of the Cold War. And yet, many men in high places in government and many who mold public opinion in the press and on the airwaves subscribe to a theory that we are at peace, and we must make no overt move which might endanger that peace. "Men cry peace, but there is no peace." The inescapable truth is that we are at war, and we are losing that war simply because we don't, or won't realize that we are in it.

Reagan knew full well the power of language "in the press and on the airwaves" to affect public opinion. His anticommunist speeches reflect this. The exciting tale of Hollywood intrigue, with monstrous communists crawling out from under rocks to try to take over Tinseltown makes for a stirring narrative. His stories are the "for instance" anecdotes that would prove his greater point. Proclaiming liberal social programs as "the foot in the door of federal control," Reagan characterized the politics and suspicions of his day as part of an apocalyptic confrontation. "There can only be one end to the war we are in," he vowed.

It won't go away if we simply try to outwait it. Wars end in victory or defeat. One of the foremost authorities on communism in the world today has said we have ten years. Not ten years to make up our minds, but ten years to win or lose—by 1970 the world will be all slave or all free.

Reagan's eight years of acting as the voice of General Electric ended in 1962. An executive from the company's advertising office told Reagan to change the subject of his pitch from politics to the virtues of General Electric appliances. Convinced that the organizations which had booked him two years in advance wanted tough politics and not tributes to toasters, Reagan quit. Within 24 hours, *GE Theater*, its ratings slipping against *Bonanza*, was cancelled and Ronald Reagan became a political free agent. Reaganites may claim that General Electric did their man an injustice when they asked him to avoid politics and then finally let him leave. It is easy to understand, though, why the company felt unwilling to support what had undeniably changed from a public relations program into an ideological polemic.

Reagan's recollections of his last months in General Electric's employ convey a pervading sense of defensiveness and of his adoption of a new persona in response to what he perceived as persecution. He had good reasons to feel assailed. Along with undisguised opposition from some General Electric officials, he found himself denounced by others outside of the company. A group of teachers in St. Paul called for their school district to prevent him from speaking to students, and popular columnist Drew Pearson singled him out for criticism as a right-winger. Reagan's account of the events surrounding his dismissal by General Electric reveals something about how he began to see himself as the hero of a quasi-literary adventure. In *Where's the Rest of Me?* he compared himself to Whittaker Chambers, "the tragic and lonely" man who "took up [his] little sling and aimed at Communism . . [and hit] that great Socialist revolution which [went by] the name of *liberalism*."[18] By comparing himself to Chambers (who seemed to Reagan a figure out of the Old Testament), Reagan characterized himself as a political David about to take on the liberal Goliath. Reagan found in Chambers—whom he mentions frequently in speeches throughout the years (and whom we will discuss in Chapter Four)—an archetypal model for his new political role.

The year that he left General Electric, Reagan joined the Republican party. He had supported Richard Nixon in 1960, and did so once more in the 1962 race against California Governor Edmund Brown, his own future opponent. Drawing on years in front of film and television cameras and on nearly a decade of speaking to factory workers, civic associations, and business groups, Reagan stumped tirelessly for his new party. In 1964, convinced that Lyndon Johnson's Great Society could mean the end of American freedom, he became cochairman of California Citizens for Goldwater, and put the famous Reagan voice to work for the right. "The Speech" was ready.

"I am going to talk of controversial things," Reagan began on October 27, 1964; "I make no apology for this." Speaking in the familiar tones of a beleaguered prophet, Reagan decried internecine quarrels that could weaken the nation at a time of crisis, then called on true Americans to unite in a struggle against "the most dangerous enemy ever known to man"—Marxism. "If we lose that war," Reagan warned, "and in so doing lose our freedom, it has been said that history will record with the greatest astonishment that those who had the most to lose did the least to prevent its happening." America, according to Ronald Reagan in 1964, should be a land with very little federal governing and a great deal of free enterprise. He cast liberals as fallen angels who had crept into the American paradise of limited government. "The real destroyer of the liberties of the people," he said (quoting Plutarch), "is he who spreads among them bounties, donations and benefits." Reagan ran through a long list of federal programs that he saw destroying our character and weakening us for the battle against tyranny. "Already the hour is late," he said; "Government has laid its hand on health, housing, farming, industry, commerce, education, and, to an ever-increasing degree interferes with the people's right to know." His speech read like an agenda against that espoused during the Roosevelt years. The Tennessee Valley Authority—"considered above criticism, sacred as motherhood"—was top on his list of evils along with housing programs, Social Security, plans to provide jobs for teenagers, the United Nations, foreign aid, governmental bureaucracy, and the banning of school prayer. "The Speech" raged against the spectrum of liberal beliefs.

The speech "A Time for Choosing" consists largely of a series of anecdotes and characterizations. Heroes and villains abound in this series of tales about America and the world on the brink of an epic ideological denouement. Reagan used some facts and figures to back up his points, but the real force of the oration comes from the "for instance" stories that put things more simply and pointedly. Audiences heard of what America meant to the world by way of a reported conversation: "Not long ago two friends of mine were talking to a Cuban refugee," this story began. Another story showed the dangers of federal housing programs. "In one key Eastern city a man owning a blighted area sold his property to Urban Renewal for several million dollars," said Reagan. "At the same time, he submitted his own plan for the rebuilding of this area and the government sold him back his own property for 22 percent of what they paid." On welfare: "Recently a judge told me of an incident in his court. A fairly young woman with six children, pregnant with her seventh, came to him for a divorce." When the judge learned that her husband opposed the separation, he questioned the woman and "the whole story came out." The divorce was a scam to cheat the government out of undeserved welfare support. And in Reagan's speech the folly of governmental red tape boils down to the following:

There are now two and one-half million federal employees. No one knows what they all do. One Congressman found out what one of them does. This man sits at a desk in Washington. Documents come to him each morning. He reads them, initials them, and passes them on to the proper agency. One day a document arrived he wasn't supposed to read, but he read it, initialled it, and passed it on. Twenty-four hours later it arrived back at his desk with a memo attached that said, "You weren't supposed to read this. Erase your initials, and initial the erasure."

The President still tells this story to the great amusement of audiences who presumably regale in this "common-sense" deflation of the government's genius for make-work.

None of Reagan's exemplary tales could be traced or disputed. Rather than provide names, dates, and other details that could be checked and then either confirmed or denied, Reagan used concrete yet evidently apocryphal vignettes to make his points. The tale of the desk-jockeying bureaucrat, for example, has no real evidence behind it. We do not learn the Congressman's name in the anecdote above, nor the man's identity, nor that of his agency. Such details would be irrelevant, even counterproductive. Reagan sought to attack not individuals, but the government in general as a creature grown fat and foolish under liberal administrations. The great puzzle of just exactly "what they all do" in Washington finds its answer in this miniscule but rhetorically powerful anecdote. Reagan shows us the bureaucrat at his desk; from that image we can extrapolate to a broader vision, imagining thousands of identical scenes until the entire federal government becomes nothing but an exercise in folly and incompetence. The story provides no proof whatsoever, but it does offer potent confirmation to listeners already convinced of its message.

"A Time for Choosing" places all of the brief anecdotes within the larger context of a struggle between good and evil, the conflict of the United States and the Soviet Union. Effective though the liberal villains of his vignettes might be, they pale compared to Reagan's depiction of the Soviets. Having opened his speech by warning that America faced in communism "the most dangerous enemy ever known to man"—a description that in religious terms applies to the devil—Reagan went on to characterize the Soviet strategy in a way recalling the Puritan poet John Milton's explanation of how Satan and his legions would use devious means to undo God's paradise:

> either with Hell-fire
> To waste his whole Creation, or possess
> All as our own, and drive as we were driven,
> The puny habitants, or if not drive,
> Seduce them to our Party . . . .

Just as, according to Milton, Satan tempted Eve and, through Eve, Adam, and then all humanity, with a sweet-tasting apple, so might Marxists undermine America's ideological paradise. Quoting Lyndon Johnson's promise that the federal government would take money "from the have's and give it to the have-not's who need it so much," Reagan translated Democratic policies into the Marxist dictum "from each according to his ability, to each according to his need," then warned Americans to "resist the *temptation* to get a government handout." Again he set Marxism up as a much more than human villainy. "We are faced with the most evil enemy mankind has known in his long climb from the swamp to the stars." Communists and their unwitting liberal allies threatened to do more than encumber us with paperwork, even more than destroy civil rights. Karl Marx appears in Reagan's speech as a fiendish anti-Christ bent on undoing God's plan for humankind.

Reagan concluded his speech by transforming the election of 1964 into one of many particular battles belonging to the eternal conflict between good and evil, other crucial moments of which included the exodus of the Jews from Egypt under Moses, Christ's sacrifice on the cross, and the battle of Concord Bridge in 1776. "APPEASEMENT OR COURAGE?" asked Reagan, invoking the terrible memory of how another force perceived as Satanic nearly conquered the world. He presented American voters a moral ultimatum. "The spectre our well-meaning liberal friends refuse to face is that their policy of accommodation is appeasement, and appeasement does not give you a choice between peace and war, only between fight and surrender." A vote for the Democrats would only help the demonic legions and Marxism to infiltrate and destroy the Republican American paradise from within:

Some of our own have said "Better Red than dead." If we are to believe that nothing is worth the dying, when did this begin? Should Moses have told the children of Israel to live in slavery rather than dare the wilderness? Should Christ have refused the Cross? Should the patroits at Concord Bridge have refused to fire the shot heard 'round the world? Are we to believe that all the martyrs of history died in vain?

Reagan placed the United States squarely in a vision of divinely ordained progress. Each heroic moment represented an historic crux from one epoch to another, moving steadily on to a holy political perfection or its civil variant. Reagan translated talk of appeasement or coexistence and of liberal social programs into blasphemous heresies in the ideological religion of conservatism. He made the sacrifices of the Republican party in the campaign of 1964, and the willingness of the American people to die rather than to tolerate the evils of Marxist government, into the moral equivalent of Christ's Crucifixion.

Reagan concluded "A Time for Choosing" by quoting with a new interpretation the words of two political leaders—Franklin Delano Roosevelt and Abraham Lincoln (two of the strongest defenders that centralized government has ever known). "You and I have a rendezvous with destiny," he told Americans;

We can preserve for our children this, the last best hope of man on earth, or we can sentence them to take the first step into a thousand years of darkness. If we fail, at least let our children and our children's children say of us we justified our brief moment here. We did all that could be done.

"The Speech" resounded with a sense of dramatic intensity. Roosevelt told delegates to the Democratic National Convention in 1936 that their generation had "a rendezvous with destiny" and called on them to preserve and to extend the New Deal, thereby making them part of his own rhetorical vision of progress under cosmic ordinance. Lincoln held up the federal government as the sacred constitutional palladium, the demise of which would mean the end of humanity's grand progress to freedom. Twisting the words of Roosevelt and Lincoln in 1964, Ronald Reagan offered a horrific millennium of communist and fascist tyranny— "a thousand years of darkness"—as the inescapable alternative to a Goldwater presidency. He turned the political contests of the 1960s into apocalyptic Armageddons. "A Time for Choosing"

took a deliberate form, the unfinished tale. Its happy or cata-
strophic ending depended entirely on how well the audience read
the story and on their willingness to see it as more than metaphor. To overcome the Satanic Marx, to escape from the enslave-
ment promised by liberalism, Americans had to accept Barry
Goldwater—and later Ronald Reagan—as their political Moses
and Messiah. With its metaphoric parables, biblical tropes, and
prospects of eternity, "A Time for Choosing" was a polemical
epic of nationalism. Although failing in its immediate goal of
defeating Lyndon Johnson, the speech nevertheless had a profound and lasting efect on the American political scene. Even as
Barry Goldwater crashed in defeat at the polls, conservatives
found a champion in this new spokesman. For years Ronald
Reagan had travelled the country, experimenting with speeches
and gradually crafting the address that in 1964 made him a genuine national political figure. He learned his rhetorical lessons
well. The man who once invented baseball games and who could
slip "in some weird way" into movie characters, and who then
fled Hollywood to escape becoming "a colored shadow" had written his own most powerful script and had found the greatest
audience with which he would ever be "together." The Voice of
the Cubs became the Great Communicator and approached his
own rendezvous with destiny.

NOTES

1. Ronald Reagan and Richard G. Hubler, *Where's the Rest of Me?* (New York: Duell, Sloan, and Pearce, 1965), p. 28.
2. Roger Rosenblatt, *Time*, January 5, 1981; cited by Lou Cannon, *Reagan* (New York: Putnam, 1982), p. 45.
3. Myrtle Moon Williams, in Cannon, op. cit., p. 46.
4. Cannon, op. cit., p. 46.
5. Cannon, op. cit., p. 45.
6. Reagan and Hubler, op. cit., p. 6.
7. Reagan and Hubler, op. cit., p. 6.
8. Cannon, op. cit., p. 73.

9. Cannon, op. cit., pp. 83–84, citing House Un-American Affairs Committee testimony of October, 1947.
10. Cannon, op. cit., p. 94, citing interview with Reagan of October 1968.
11. Reagan and Hubler, op. cit., p. 258.
12. Reagan and Hubler, op. cit., p. 263.
13. Reagan and Hubler, op. cit., pp. 266–67.
14. William E. Leuchtenberg, *In the Shadow of FDR: from Harry Truman to Ronald Reagan* (Ithaca, N.Y.: Cornell University Press, 1983), p. 233; Leuchtenberg's chapter on Reagan is an especially good treatment of Reagan's shift from liberalism to conservatism.
15. Reagan and Hubler, op. cit., p. 264.
16. Cannon, op. cit., p. 95, citing an interview with Reagan of July 30, 1981.
17. Reagan and Hubler, op. cit., p. 269–70.
18. Reagan and Hubler, op. cit., p. 268.

3 / ANALOGIES, ALLEGORIES, AND HOMILIES

The strategy of mixing expository argument with allegorical narrative that we found in "A Time for Choosing" runs throughout Reagan's oratory. One of his most common phrases is "There's a story . . . ," introducing bits of history, instances of pseudohistory, jokes, excerpts from letters, folktales, and other exempla designed to give life to Reagan's principles. Tales of courage, piety, charity, idealism, and the many virtues of Americans as well as the vices of their foes abound in his work. Recalling to us his concerns that Hollywood films could be used for communist propaganda, the President has on several occasions told a story about storytelling: "There's been a lot of talk in the last several weeks here in Washington about communication and the need to communicate," Reagan told the Building and Construction

Trades Department of the AFL-CIO in 1981. He then repeated a favorite joke "about commununication and some of the basic rules of communication," featuring a young baseball star and his wife. Preparing dinner one evening while her famous husband relaxed in the living room, the woman heard her baby start to cry.

And over her shoulder, the wife said to her husband, "Change the baby." And this young ballplayer . . . said to his wife, "What do you mean change the baby? I'm a ballplayer. That's not my line of work." And she turned around, put her hands on her hips, and she communicated. She said, "Look buster, you lay the diaper out like a diamond, you put second base on home plate, put the baby's bottom on the pitcher's mound, hook up first and third, slide home underneath, and if it starts to rain, the game ain't called, you start all over again."

"So, concluded the President, I'm going to try to communicate a little bit today." And he did so in exactly the fashion suggested by the joke: by analogy. Just as the wife used a fictive device to make her point, so the President immediately told a story to convince his carpenter audience that the federal government had to get out of construction regulation:

I've told before, I have a neighbor out in my neighborhood in California who was building his own home. And he got so fed up with all the paperwork and the regulations required that he pasted them all together into one strip of paper, put up two poles in front of the half-finished house, and strung them up across there. The strip of paper was 250 feet long.

Like the tale of the bureaucrat who initialed documents all day long, this story is virtually impossible to verify. But its veracity hardly mattered to the carpenters in Reagan's audience who had doubtless filled out their share of paperwork and whom the President assumed would identify with his neighbor.

Not all of the stories are jokes, of course, but they usually rely on an emotional appeal of one kind or another, be it humor, pride, nostalgia, or pious humility. We cannot look at all of the President's hundreds of fables and parables, but even a few can show how he "communicates." One very common story from his repertoire centers around the United States military, our foreign policy, and the role of "family values" in the American character. It recounts an episode that the President says took place in Great Britain shortly after the end of World War II. Driving around the English countryside after a day of filming, Reagan stopped at a pub run by "an elderly couple, very tiny." As her husband hovered in the background, "the rather motherly looking lady" who served Reagan recalled the American G.I.'s who had been stationed down the road during the war:

She said, "They used to come in here all the time in the evenings and have songfests." She said, "They called me Mom and the old man Pop." And as she went on her voice was softening and she wasn't looking at me anymore; she was looking kind of beyond into her memories. Her eyes were beginning to fill. And then she said, "It was Christmas Eve. The old man and me were here all alone. And all of a sudden the door burst open, and in they came with presents for the both of us." And the tears now had overflowed and were on her cheeks. And she said, "Big strappin' lads they was from a place called Ioway." By this time my eyes were a little filled also.

Frequently appearing in Reagan's repertoire the story played an especially important part in the speech that Mr. Reagan gave to the Corn Growers Association in 1982. It reached out to the audience in several ways. One had to do with those in the audience being gathered in Iowa, the putative home of the farm-boy soldiers. This circumstance allowed Reagan to celebrate not just American heroes, but even to suggest that some of those "big strappin' lads" might have been in his audience that very day. Another theme of the anecdote is the ever-present Reagan paean to the family. Set on a date redolent with sentimental familial associations, Christmas Eve, the story presents a brief familial

34

drama in which our soldiers are good boys, who respect their elders, and who would never dream of letting even a surrogate parent go unloved. We find, too, the President's oft-repeated theme of volunteerism. The soldiers took it upon themselves to cheer up the old folks; no federal agency or company commander had to tell them to act generously.

And finally we find in the story an allegory of American foreign policy. England is, after all, the mother country of the United States, so the filial response of the soldiers to the old couple seems oddly fitting. This loyalty has an edge of chauvinistic patronism, though, that may bother us if we consider what the President's story tells us about how the rest of the world appears to America. The tired and lonely old people are "very tiny," utterly helpless even to mark Christmas Eve (and England, after all, is the home of the Dickensian Christmas in the American imagination) without the help of the emphatically "big strappin'" Americans. The subtextual message seems to be that, while we should use our national abundance and strength to help the world, we should also remember that other nations remain decidedly our inferiors. Finally, the episode establishes Reagan as a special representative of the United States; it was to him that the old woman recounted her memory. Of course, her story was only part of Reagan's bigger story. We hear not just her recollection, but his memory of their meeting. His sentimental self-characterization serves as an example to the audience, whose own eyes should be filling with tears. And, finally, we have the story of America under Reagan's presidency, an administration dedicated to restoring the United States (especially in military terms) to a position of prestige like that testified to by the old woman's almost pathetic gratitude. Looked at cynically, this image of strength is hardly pleasant, but when interpreted through the narrative persona of the President, its ugly aspects disappear.

We can also see how Reagan uses stories within stories to reinforce his public self in a tale that he frequently tells ostensibly to

35

show humanity's dependence on God. Reagan told this "story by an unknown author, a story of a dream he had" to a White House prayers meeting in 1982. He had used the same story a year earlier, just before his near assassination:

He had dreamt, as you recall, that he walked down the beach beside the Lord. And as they walked, above him in the sky was reflected each experience of his life. And then reaching the end of the beach, he looked back and saw the two sets of footprints extending down the way, but suddenly noticed that every once in a while there was only one set of footprints. And each time, they were opposite a reflection in the sky of a time of great trial and suffering in his life. And he turned to the Lord in surprise and said, "You promised that if I walked with You, You would always be by my side. Why did you desert me in my times of need?" And the Lord said, "My beloved child, I wouldn't desert you when you needed Me. When you see only one set of footprints, it was then that I carried you."

The President then made a special point of relating his own travails to the story: "[T]here came a moment when, without doubt, I was carried." This kind of homily has enormous popular appeal in America, reinforcing the President's commitment to religious issues such as school prayer and abortion—positions that have brought him millions of votes and campaign dollars and also the support of highly skilled political action organizations. The pious story outlines Reagan's understanding of how life works in this world. Ultimate moral power and responsibility resides not in our own hands nor in those of our elected governments, but in the will and mercy of God.

At the same time, Reagan's gratitude for God's protection is by extension an implicit claim of his blessing and of his commission, a confirmation that Reagan was in fact doing God's work: "I've always believed that we were, each of us, put here for a reason," he concluded, "that there is a plan, somehow a divine plan for all of us. I know now that whatever days are left to me belong to Him." God saved the President "for a reason"; Reagan's remaining days "belong to Him." The moral of the story is that God has chosen and protected Ronald Reagan for the sake of some divine mission. On its own, the dream vision of the man on the beach expresses its author's belief in humanity's dependence on God. But as Reagan told the tale and put it in the context of his politics and shooting, and into the history of his own life and near death, he turned it into a metaphor for *his* life, transforming himself from the reader of the original story into a hero of his own version of it. The story of the dream was but a prologue to his own tale of divine significance.

Another instance of the use of the story suggests that Reagan has not entirely given up depending on scripts written by others. The simple tale of Reagan's pride in the American people and their willingness to serve in the military is one that the President has been using for years and years in many settings. It comes from a national television address of July 6, 1976:

[At the time when prisoners of war were returning to America from Vietnam] Nancy and I were to share an experience that will live in our hearts forever. We were permitted to offically welcome more than 250 [Californian POW's] as guests in our home. . . . It was an unforgettable and inspiring experience. . . . One night after our guests had gone and Nancy and I were alone, I asked, "Where did we find them, where did we find such men?" The answer came to me almost as quickly as I'd asked the question. We found them where we've always found them when such men are needed—on Main Street, on our farms, in shops and stores, in offices, oil stations, and factories. They are simply the product of the freest society man has ever known.

This heart-swelling reminiscence apparently depicts a very personal moment in President Reagan's life, a moment when he was sincerely touched by the heroic and virtuous men who had suffered on behalf of freedom. On one level it works as a model, of course, for how Reagan would like his countrymen to feel about the soldiers, the Vietnam War, and themselves. On another, it presents the President as a courageously sentimental man whose almost embarrassingly sincere words and emotions express the heart of the country. Ronald Reagan did believe strongly in the American government's involvement in Vietnam, and no doubt the episode does capture his own convictions. The curious thing about the story, though, is that even while he seemed to be baring his own heart, the President was in fact borrowing words from James Michener's novel of historical fiction *The Bridges at Toko-Ri*. Speaking to the crew of the *U.S.S. Constellation* in 1981 off the coast of Korea, Reagan cited Michener's book:

[I]n the final scene of the book, Michener writes of the admiral, standing on the darkened bridge of his carrier, waiting for the pilots who had flown off the carrier's deck that day to bomb the Toko-Ri bridges. . . . The admiral wondered at their selflessness, standing there alone in the darkness, and then in the book he asked aloud, "Where do we get such men?"[1]

Adapting the wartime meditation of Michener's anticommunist Admiral Tarrant to the circumstances of his own troops, Commander-in-Chief Reagan told the crew of the *Constellation*, "Well, you're the answer to that question. Those men he was speaking of came from cities and towns [etc.]. . . ." Reagan (or his speechwriters) certainly didn't *plagiarize* his moving silent question. We might note, though, how comfortably the President slipped into the fictive world, becoming once again "a colored shadow" living somewhere between reality and imagination, and paraphrasing the words of a novelist as if he were himself a character in the book.

One of the most extended instances of Reagan's manipulation of himself, his audience, and a text occurs in his 1981 commencement address at Notre Dame. An unusually important speech for Reagan, this was the President's first appearance at Notre Dame since taking office as well as the most widely covered event on his first trip away from the Capitol after being shot. Notre Dame has powerful associations for Reagan because he played the Gipper in *Knute Rockne—All American*. Packed with meaning for Reagan's personal drama, the Notre Dame address stands as probably the single most revealing and important illustration of Reagan's fictive technique.

The film portrayed the life of Norwegian immigrant Knute Rockne, who coached the Notre Dame football team from 1918 to 1931. With the Great Depression looming on the horizon, the string of brilliant victories to which Rockne led his team raised spirits across America. Reagan told the class of 1981 how his youthful hero affected him.

Growing up in Illinois, I was influenced by a sports legend so national in scope, it was almost mystical. It is difficult to explain to anyone who didn't live in those times. The legend was based on a combination of three elements: a game, football; a university, Notre Dame; and a man, Knute Rockne. There has been nothing like it before or since.

Reagan's fondness for Rockne came naturally, stemming from his own participation in high school and college football, which, he confesses, was one of the great passions of his life. When he left sports broadcasting to enter the film industry, Reagan carried with him a lifelong love of athletics and an abiding admiration for its great heroes. One of the future President's earliest breaks as an actor came when he learned that Warner Brothers planned to make a movie of Rockne's life. The studio had tested ten actors for the part of George Gipp, the young player who died in school and reportedly uttered the famous last words, "Tell them to win one for the Gipper." On the strength of his athletic knowledge, and a recommendation from Pat O'Brien, who played Knute, Reagan got the part. As he tells it, the role came his way by an almost miraculous coincidence:

Having come from the world of sports, I'd been trying to write a story about Knute Rockne. I must confess that I had someone [i.e., himself] in mind to play the Gipper. On one of my sports broadcasts before going to Hollywood, I had told the story of his career and tragic death. I didn't have very many words on paper when I learned that the studio that employed me was already preparing a story treatment for that film.

Even before learning of Warner Brothers' scheme, Reagan was bent on writing himself into the story of George Gipp.[2] In fact, Reagan's Gipp has entirely replaced the historical figure who inspired it. If not for Ronald Reagan, hardly anyone would remember Gipp today. So pervasive is the identification of Reagan with Gipp that when he ran against Carter in 1980, some people were surprised to learn that Reagan had not actually attended Notre Dame himself. Other presidents had spoken at Notre Dame, but none seemed so fitting as Reagan.

On its surface, Reagan's speech is a typical college graduation talk, mingling nostalgia with happy prospects, sentiment with cautions and encouragements in the time-tested manner. Jimmy Carter had spoken at Notre Dame during his term in office and announced some policy matters; Reagan said that he wanted to avoid politics and pronouncements, but like any successful politician he was not about to let an opportunity go to waste. He wove a good bit of politics into the memories and promises—a combination which should not surprise us from a speaker who so comfortably blends his ideological messages into all sorts of rhetorical contexts.

We know that Rockne and the Gipper meant much to Reagan; he described their effect as preternatural, and viewed it as an allegory for American history. "Now I'm going to mention again that movie that Pat and I and Notre Dame [the film was actually made entirely in California] were in," Reagan said, "because it says something about America." Rockne is more than a coach who could win ball games. He is an archetypal American hero:

First, Knute Rockne as a boy came to America with his parents from Norway. And in the few years it took him to grow up to college age, he became so American that here at Notre Dame, he became an All American in a game that is still, to this day, uniquely American.

The designation "All American" refers to the fact that players on a team so designated are chosen from across the country, from all of America; in the sense in which the title strictly applies to Rockne, therefore, it means literally "one of America's best." A secondary meaning has eclipsed the original significance, and Reagan had this definition in mind. Despite his foreign birth, Rockne was Americanized quickly and completely. Behaving in a thoroughly American way (by playing a uniquely American game and by winning aggressively), he became a symbolic archetype for Reagan's patriotic vision. The President extended his redefinition of "All American" to include activities that went far beyond the immediate concerns of football, including one close to Reagan's heart and to his task in the speech: moral inspiration.

As a coach, [Rockne] did more than teach young men how to play a game. He believed truly that the noblest work of man was building the character of man. And maybe that's why he was a living legend. No man connected with football has ever achieved the stature or occupied the singular niche in the Nation that he carved out for himself, not just in a sport, but in our entire social structure.

Rockne earned adulation for winning football games, but Reagan prefers to remember him for shaping the characters of his young charges. In Reagan's interpretation, the coach acted as a kind of father figure for America, much in the same way that real-life coaches sometimes do for individual players. The film moves at a disturbingly quick pace through Rockne's victories and occasional setbacks; in their haste to get on with the story, the producers actually devoted very little footage to any real character building on the part of Rockne. We see him appropriately playful and stern with his team as circumstances demand, but nothing especially remarkable is revealed in his dealings with players. As retold by Reagan, however, the story of Knute Rockne is that of a man who put the nurturance of his followers' hearts and minds ahead of gridiron victories and who ultimately achieved those very victories through his attentions to the players' faith in themselves. The story of Knute Rockne is a dramatic projection of Reagan's own quest to inspire the American people anew.

During his life, Rockne's most famous players were probably the four backfielders called collectively *"The Four Horsemen"*—an echo of the Four Horsemen of the Apocalypse in the Book of Revelations. Thanks to the Reagan and O'Brien movie version, though, George Gipp is the player whom we remember best. In honest fact, George Gipp was something of a hell raiser, hardly a devout admirer of Rockne's moralisms. As portrayed by young Reagan, though, Gipp was a model player, his sharp edges blunted and his spare time spent at the Rockne homestead. A star on the gridiron who seemed not to know what the word "impossible" meant, Reagan's Gipper combined boyish eagerness with a knack for open-field running. Gipp died, as anyone who saw the film knows, before graduation. On his deathbed he asked Coach Rockne to pass his last request on to the squad, "Tell them," he gasped, "to win one for the Gipper."[3] Rockne kept Gipp's dying wish to himself for eight years, holding the exhortation from beyond the grave until a moment of extreme crisis. Reagan—now speaking as a narrator—interpreted:

But let's look at the *significance of that story.* Rockne could have used Gipp's dying words to win a game any time. But 8 years went by following the death of George Gipp before Rock revealed those dying words, his deathbed wish.

And then he told the story at halftime to a team that was losing, and one of the only teams he had ever coached that was torn by dissention and jealously [sic] and factionalism. The seniors on that team were about to close out their football careers without learning or experiencing any of the real values that a game has to impart. None of them had known George Gipp. They were children when he played for Notre Dame. It was to this team that Rockne told the story and so inspired them that they rose above their personal animosities. For someone they had never known, they joined together in a common cause and attained the unattainable. [My italics.]

In other words, Rockne turned Gipp and his dying words into a rhetorical symbol that he used to inspire loyalty.

A seemingly gratuitous digression on Winston Churchill provides the central theme of Reagan's speech and the clue to how he wants us to read his story of Rockne and Gipp:

Winston Churchill, during the darkest period of the "Battle of Britain" in World War II said: "When great causes are on the move in the world . . . we learn we are spirits, not animals, and that something is going on in space and time, and beyond space and time, which, whether we like it or not, spells duty."

When Knute Rockne invoked the name and words of the dead Gipper, he used them as a rhetorical device. "Someone they had never known" [Gipp] functioned as "something beyond space and time" [Churchill's source of duty]. This invocation brought harmony and victory to the squad. It is important to realize that the response came not to George Gipp the real (albeit departed) person, but to the Unknown Player—an abstract hero from the past who stood for much more than just the facts of his life. Gipp sent his last message to the young men with whom he himself had actually played. But Rockne used Gipp's dying words for a related although really quite separate purpose. He turned the Gipper into a myth. The device worked; the team won, according to Reagan. As one player who scored was carried injured off the field, he was heard to say, "That's the last one I can get for you, Gipper." Reagan drew a moral for the class of 1981:

Now it's only a game. And . . . it might sound maudlin. . . . But is there anything wrong with young people having an experience, feeling something so deeply, thinking of someone else to the point that they can give so completely of themselves? There will come times in the lives of all of us when we'll be faced with causes bigger than ourselves, and they won't be on a playing field.

It was a touching story, one well designed to stir Reagan's

audience on a sentimental occasion. But consider how far rhetoric moved from reality. The tale began with the events of Rockne's and Gipp's actual lives. Then it underwent a Hollywood "story treatment," in turn reinterpreted by the various creative members of the production company, that is, the director, designers, and the actors themselves (none of whom knew the real people on whom their characters were based). Finally, the whole thing was changed again by Reagan and his speechwriters. This evolution transformed history into a powerful set of cinematic symbols (representing the values and beliefs of Warner Brothers more honestly than those of Rockne or Gipp) and then made the film into an allegory for Reagan's message to Americans. In his halftime speech to the losing team, Rockne made a symbol of Gipp; and Hollywood went on to make a new symbol out of that first rhetorical act. Reagan carried the process a step farther, moving even farther from factuality. Basing his speech not on historical fact, but on an undeniably fictionalized "treatment," he revived the cinemagraphic symbol of 1940 and applied it to the concerns of 1981 as he presented them in his own presidential pep rally. Just as Rockne resurrected Gipp to inspire his team, so did Reagan create a drama to move his own audience in 1981.

With an emotional backdrop in place for the rest of the speech, Reagan abruptly turned from football and movies to American history. "This Nation," he told the graduates,

was born when a band of men, the Founding Fathers, a group so unique we've never seen their like since, rose to such selfless heights [as those exemplified by Rockne's team]. . . . [These 56 men] pledged their lives, their fortunes, and their sacred honor. 16 of them gave their lives. Most gave their fortunes. All preserved their sacred honor.

Rockne's comeback team succeeded only because they recognized their communal heritage of the inspiring example left by the Gipper. Of the government that the Founding Fathers designed and left for posterity, Reagan told the new graduates, "This

44

is the heritage that you're about to claim as you come out to join the society made up of those who have preceded you. . . ." In a sense—and if the metaphor seems ludicrous, it nevertheless has potency in a society that elevates its athletic heroes as much as we do—the Founding Fathers are the Grand Gippers of the United States. The signers of the Declaration of Independence also resemble Knute Rockne. Just as Knute put character building above mere scores, so did the Founding Fathers give us "more than a nation":

They brought to all mankind for the first time the concept that man was born free, that each of us has inalienable rights, ours by the grace of God, and that government was created by us for our convenience, having only the powers that we chose to give it.

The sense of history is important. In telling his story about football, Reagan first established himself as an authoritive spokesman for the past. As the alter ego of George Gipp, didn't he know the story and its meaning better than anyone else ever could have? (Better, in fact, than even the scriptwriter or Gipp himself could have?) And the past which President Reagan interpreted demanded respect. Rockne's team had to take Gipp's dying words seriously. So did the class of 1981 depend on Reagan's speech. The President carried the lessons of Rockne's game-saving exhortation into his vision of America. The past matters. We need to rely on it for our guidance as we approach the future. This position, the most basic premise of Anglo-American conservatism, underlies all of Reagan's politics.

Reagan paused for a moment after celebrating the Founding Fathers to praise American progress, and in doing so he employed yet another artistic metaphor. Suggesting that if the entire history of the world could be put on film (presumably without a "story treatment") and projected within 24 hours, the United States would rise only in the last three and a half seconds, Reagan called our accomplishments "Such miracles of invention, con-

45

struction, and production as the world has never seen." He echoed again his statement that "there has been nothing like [Rockne and his accomplishments] before or since." But just as one of Rockne's teams fell into discord and despair, Americans in Reagan's view had for a time dangerously abandoned the dream and wisdom of their forefathers. Noting the poor state of the American economy in 1981—a circumstance that he blamed on the Democrats—Reagan said,

You know, we who had preceded you had just gotten so busy that we let things get out of hand. We forgot that we were the keepers of the power, forgot to challenge the notion that the state is the principal vehicle of social change, forgot that millions of social interactions among free individuals and institutions can do more to foster economic and social progress than all the careful schemes of government planners.

Reagan sounded like Coach Rockne at halftime, rallying the lackluster team that had forgotten how to pull together. And true to the peptalk pattern of the speech, encouragement followed criticism. "Well, at last we're remembering," said the President in an obvious reference to his own election on a platform to reduce government.

Speaking as America's coach, Reagan appealed to the class of 1981:

We need you. We need your youth. We need your strength. We need your idealism to help us make right that which is wrong. Now, I know that this period of your life, you have been and are critically looking at the mores and customs of the past and questioning their value. Every generation does that. May I suggest, don't discard the time-tested values upon which civilization was built simply because they're old? More important, don't let today's doom criers and cynics persuade that the best is past, that from here on it's all downhill.

"Get out there and give 'em all you've got," Reagan seemed to say. He called on his young audience to "win one for the Gipper" in two senses: for the Gipper first as a symbol of past greatness that ought to inspire future effort, and again for that other more tangible Gipper, Ronald Reagan himself, a man determined that the future should preserve the perceived glories of the past.

The doom criers and cynics out to destroy American confidence and deny Reagan's vision are the trouble makers who nearly pulled Rockne's team apart. Just as he warned audiences in the 1960s that they had to act at once in order to prevent a millenium of darkness, so Reagan insisted that 1981 was a crucial turning point in history. Whether speaking at halftime or "a time for choosing," Reagan made his audience leading characters in the grand drama of history.

Reagan then looked to America's future, the second half of the great football game of history. If Americans would heed his words, they could pull together, remedy the internal strife of the pre-Reagan years, and could defeat the opposing team—Soviet Marxists. "The years ahead are great ones for this country," he prophesied, "for the cause of freedom and the spread of civilization. The West won't contain communism, it will transcend communism." Reagan quoted words of William Faulkner, lines recalling the kind of moral advice that Rockne gave players: in "the old verities and truths of the heart" lie our hopes. Man, Reagan quoted, "is immortal because he alone among creatures . . . has a soul, a spirit capable of compassion and sacrifice and endurance." Just as character made the crucial difference in Notre Dame's football games, so could virtue and faith save the world for the American Dream. The possibility that such moral qualities might exist among the citizens of the Soviet Union has no place in this black-and-white vision—no more than kind or respectful words for the opposing team would belong in a real college pep rally. (Chants of "Kill 'em, stomp 'em, knock 'em dead" come to mind.) *Our* team, *our* nation alone has the kind of character that brings victory. Deprived of moral leaders like Rockne, Washington, and Reagan himself the Russians represent at best a "bizarre chapter in human history whose last pages are even now being written." Reagan delivered a grand halftime

47

speech for American youth, one for which he chose all the characters and situations. Reagan identified the opponents, described the grim situation into which his own side was falling, and rhetorically linked those Americans who rejected his policies with the opposing communist team.

Drawing to the conclusion of his speech, Reagan gave his listeners a final rallying cry:

> For the West, for America, the time has come to dare to show to the world that our civilized ideas, our traditions, our values, are not—like the ideology and war machine of totalitarian societies—just a facade of strength. It is time for the world to know our intellectual and spiritual values are rooted in the source of all strength, a belief in a Supreme Being, and a law higher than our own.

Just as Rockne put more stock in character building than in gridiron victories, so the President put moral conviction above mere military power. (Of course, he omitted the fact that Rockne won his reputation in the first place by developing a devastating offensive strategy that relied on the ballistic forward pass.)

America and its allies can win the great game because of their belief in God and in some higher law—objects equivalent to Gipper as the Unknown Player and to Churchill's "something beyond space and time." America will win, in other words, because Coach Great Communicator will keep us true to the right team spirit.

As the Gipper, Reagan had learned the lesson of unity in the face of strife, and in his last words passed that wisdom on to his teammates. Speaking as America's President, Reagan took on the part of Coach Rockne. He cast the class of 1981 as a new generation of players who would one day have to coach their own descendants. Like Reagan, the graduates have a duty to keep the legends of history alive and properly interpreted:

> My hope today is that in the years to come and come it shall—when it's your time explain to another generation the meaning of the past and

thereby hold out to them the promise of their future, that you'll recall the truths and traditions of which we've spoken. It is these truths and traditions that define our civilization and make up our national heritage. And now, they're yours to protect and pass on.

The assumption in the passage above is that all that Reagan has said is "truth." But the mechanics of the speech undermine this premise. The "truths and traditions" are the morals that Reagan had drawn from his fictive parable. Reagan has made an interpretation of history based not on facts, but on metaphor, on acting and on story treatments. Reagan's didactic history of the world is not history, but consciously crafted mythology. He played the part of not just a man elected to an administrative post for a limited time, but of the latest in a series of prophet-coaches. The dramatis personae and points of view in the speech are jumbled together. Reagan becomes both the Gipper and Rockne, coach and player, father and loyal son. The President stepped "beyond space and time" to embody the lesson of history.

The Notre Dame address exemplifies superbly how President Reagan moves rhetorically back and forth between fiction and the real world. On the one hand, he makes himself a hero of his own tales, substituting for reality the epic adventures and homely folktales of his oratory. Just as Reagan appears in his stories as America's symbolic ambassador abroad in an English pub, the annointed of God at a prayer breakfast, the Gipper, or Rockne, so does the United States of America change into something more poetic than realistic. The events of history translate into a walk on the beach with the Lord, or a football game on the brink of disaster for the home team. Believing in Reagan's words, we, too, become "colored shadows."

NOTES

1. Michener's exact words are:

Reagan Speaks

For many hours the admiral remained alone. Then toward morning he heard the anti-submarine patrol go out and as the engines roared he asked "Why is America lucky enough to have such men? They leave this tiny ship and fly against the enemy. Then they must seek the ship, lost somewhere on the sea. And when they find it, they have to land on its pitching deck. Where did we get such men?

James A. Michener, *The Bridges at Toko-Ri* (New York: Random House, 1953), p. 146.

2. Robert Dalleck, *Ronald Reagan: The Politics of Symbolism* (Cambridge: Harvard University Press, 1984), p. 20.

3. This scene, curiously, did not appear in the single print of *Kunte Rockne—All-American* that I have seen. I gather, however, that the print had been heavily edited. Reagan reports that the scene does appear in the film. Ronald Reagan and Richard C. Hubler, *Where's the Rest of Me?* (New York: Duell, Sloane and Pearce, 1965), p. 95.

4 / STOCK
CHARACTERS

One of Reagan's most powerful rhetorical devices is his use of stock symbolic characters. By personifying his beliefs about good and evil in simply drawn men and women, the President provides points of reference and points of view for his audience. As literary scholar M. H. Abrams puts it, "Characters are the persons presented in a dramatic or narrative work, who are interpreted by the reader as being endowed with moral and dispositional qualities that are expressed by what they say . . . and by what they do."[1] The heroes and villains of Reagan's speeches are far from realistic; they are tools through which the speaker manipulates us by translating our complicated and varied lives into simplified stock characters, two-dimensional dramatis personae embodying virtue and vice. In this regard his speeches resemble medieval morality plays, the protagonists and antagonists of which had names and even costumes to ensure that even the most unsophisticated audience could follow the moral action of the play. Medieval dramatists used this heavy-handed technique because they believed that the immortal souls of their viewers depended on how effectively they could communicate Christian doctrine, the common theme of their didactic drama. In his passage through the world, the fittingly named Everyman met friends and enemies named Fellowship, Good, Beauty, Discretion, and Death. Only through his adventures with these allegorical entities could Everyman at last follow Angel to the throne of God. While Ronald Reagan doesn't quite go so far as to give his characters such blatant names, the men and women who dwell in his oratorical political morality plays are nevertheless clearly embodiments of good and evil.

When Reagan left Hollywood to work for General Electric, he wanted to escape becoming a character himself, but as we have seen, he did not entirely succeed. At the same time, the future President sought to rediscover the real people of America, the simple folk with whom he had grown up and who differed so from the cinematic creations of scriptwriters. Even while he was creating new personas for himself as the storyteller/hero of his own story, though, Reagan set about making a cast of characters to stand for the American people in that same narrative. Reagan's homespun men and women, ostensibly pure and uncomplicated, are yet heavily colored with Reagan's ideological and emotional principles.

The President describes his own youth in idealistically sentimental terms. However, his real childhood was not the Norman Rockwellesque experience that we might think it was: by his own admission, young Reagan suffered considerable unhappiness because of his father's alcoholism and the long periods of unemployment that kept the family moving from small town to small town. Nevertheless, in creating a symbolic autobiography suitable for a potential American president, Reagan described a very different kind of childhood in harmony with his reincarnation. It was, he wrote in *Where's the Rest of Me?*:

. . . one of those rare Huck Finn-Tom Sawyer idylls. There were woods and mysteries, life and death among the small creatures, hunting and fishing; those were days when I learned the real riches of rags. . . . Waiting and hoping for the winter freeze without snow so that we could go skating on Rock River . . . swimming and picnics in the summer, the long thoughts of spring, the pain with the coloring of the falling leaves in autumn. It was a good life. I have never asked for anything more, then or now.[2]

Reagan pictured the world as a series of natural cycles, and himself in communion with the best spirits of nature. Hard times became joys: poverty, "real riches"; death, something almost pleasant among toylike "small creatures." Inverting reality to make his life allegory, the President claimed the blessing of American soil. "There was the life," he wrote, "that shaped my body and my mind for all the years to come after." (Of course, all this poetic reverie is nonsense: leaving the Midwest as fast as he could, high-tailling it to college, the city, Hollywood, Sacremento, and the White House. Reagan has many times asked for a great deal more indeed than the bucolic scenes of Dixon, Illinois.) We hear echoes of Reagan's words in his 1982 speech to the Corn Growers Association. Dismissing the work done by federal agricultural agencies, Reagan told farmers they "never needed government to tell them how to bring food for a hungry world from the blue-black soil of this heartland." From that same soil and those same homespun heroes would come the nation's salvation: "Here in the land where the west begins and the State where the tall corn grows are the seeds of our national renewal. Within our people is the strength, the vision, and the faith that will . . . set this country to rights." Disturbing details disappear altogether.

The human counterpart of such a natural environment is the family, where the instincts and lessons of God's creation take human form. "Families," the President has said many times, "are the basic unit of religious and moral values that hold our society together"; to save ourselves, he has often argued, "we must look to God [and] to the hearthstone, because that's where all hope for America lies." The family is "the cornerstone of our society," and mothers are "the heart of the family" who personify nurturance and natural piety. As he said in a Mother's Day speech of May 7, 1983:

In our families, and often from our mothers, we first learn about values and caring and the difference between right and wrong. Those of us blessed with loving families draw our confidence from them and the strength we need to face the world. We also first learn at home, and, again, often from our mothers, about the God who will guide us through life.

Nelle Reagan was by far the stronger of the President's parents. His father tended to divide the family and to undermine the youths' happiness. Nelle sheltered Reagan and his brother and kept the family together in hard times. President Reagan speaks of her often, characterizing her as the embodiment of the same kind of unsophisticated yet profound wisdom borne of humility and piety that his farmers glean from the soil. "[S]he taught us about life," said the President on Mother's Day, 1984; "She had never gone beyond . . . elementary school, but she had a different kind of education that I think has been imprinted and a faith that I know has been bestowed on me." This simple wisdom of the human heart, based on familial love and religious belief, constitutes the basic and all-essential premise of Reagan's homespun heroes. Just as his own mother taught him to love life and to believe in the power of prayer, so can the idealized mother of his rhetorical family give the country its best guidance. Even if we cannot all enjoy the close-to-the-soil nurturance that Reagan and farmers did, we can learn the same truths of our world from our mothers, who act in Reagan's speech as saintly spirits doing God's work.

We have encountered the family before in Reagan's speeches. The Iowa farm-boy soldiers who acted as loving sons to the elderly British pub owners were as much sons as they were soldiers. Children—especially sons—are also important stock characters in Reagan's dramas, appearing in a variety of particular guises, one of the most common and telling of which is the soldier. We recall the G.I.'s who brought Christmas gifts to the elderly pub owners as one such example. Reagan's May 28, 1984 Memorial Day graveside eulogy in Arlington National Cemetary for the Unknown Serviceman of the Vietnam conflict is another. Calling the soldier "symbolic of all our missing sons," the President imagined the life of the soldier before the war. "About him we may wonder as others have: As a child, did he play on some street in some great American city? Or did he work beside his father on a farm out in America's heartland?" Soldiers of all ages died in Vietnam, but Reagan made his soldier specifically a young man, the good son who carried the lessons of his family and faith abroad as the Iowa boys did to a foreign land. "Thank you, dear son," prayed the President in closing; "May God cradle you in His loving arms."

Reagan gave another address for the soldier. On May 25th, the President delivered a short speech for a Capitol Rotunda ceremony. Although it was one of the briefest speeches that Reagan has ever delivered, this funeral oration is a superb exercise in poetic characterization for a variety of specific political ends, which include defending American involvement in the Vietnam War and preparing a justification for military steps that Reagan might one day feel the need himself to take. Standing by the casket in the Capitol Rotunda, the President sought to assign a moral meaning to the Vietnam War and to extend that interpretation to explain armed conflict in general.

Like the nameless bureaucrats and disgruntled citizens of his other speeches, the Unknown Serviceman is a complete and absolute cipher, a faceless mannequin on which Reagan could draw whatever features and expressions he wished. The Arlington National Cemetery memorial was not, we might recall, the first national memorial to Vietnam veterans, nor is it the most well known. In the fall of 1982 the privately funded Vietnam Veterans Memorial Fund dedicated its somber monument: a basaltic "v" etched with nearly 60,000 names of dead soldiers. This marker commemorated strictly *known* heroes, though. Their engraved names remind visitors of actual sons and daughters, fathers and brothers who died in America's most unpopular war. Its haunting litany of the dead forever preserved for the public, the monument does not allow us to escape from painful reality. President Reagan said little to mark the dedication of that memorial, maybe because the victims of the war were too overpoweringly present and because of the strong opposition to the Vietnam War that pervaded public sentiment at the time of the dedication. He confined himself to a few words at the beginning of a long address on the folly of putting arms control before a policy of deterence. "On behalf of the nation," he said in passing, "let me again thank the Vietnam veterans from the bottom of my heart for their courageous service to America."

Finding a truly unknown soldier for the Arlington tomb was no easy job. Those in charge worked hard to provide the President with a symbolic casualty around which he could craft his rhetoric. However, medical pathologists are so skilled in identifying the dead (and medical records are so extensive) that, as the deadline drew near, two of the four corpses that were finally considered were named; the identification of a third seemed imminent. The fourth body, which was finally interred in the flag-draped coffin, must have been in truly shocking condition. To be so utterly beyond identification it had to lack not only a face and hand or foot prints but all of the other miniscule anatomical details which give clues to experts. The reality of the corpse is hideous to contemplate, as terrible as the Vietnam war was and as armed conflict in general remains for many Americans. Stripped of its horrific actuality though, and hidden ceremoniously away in a flag-bedecked casket, the charred and rotted body could act as the perfect vehicle for a message quite different from that which its actuality would convey. Had the ceremony featured an open casket, the image of the Vietnam War would hardly have fit Reagan's communicative strategy. What mattered was not the real body, not the true once-named soldier who fought and died, but the metaphoric cipher that lay in the Capitol rotunda as the President spoke.

Reagan began his eulogy by admitting his ignorance of the man's true identity and then investing him with a new symbolic identity. "An American hero has returned home," he pronounced, "God bless him."

> We may not know of this man's life, but we know of his character. We may not know his name, but we know his courage. He is the heart, the spirit, the soul of America.

Ignorance, if not blissful, is certainly utilitarian. As "the heart, the spirit, and the soul" of the country, the reincarnated soldier represents the essence of the American people as the President believes us—or wants us—to be. By speaking of the burial as a homecoming, Reagan ritualistically reconciled post-Vietnam America with those impulses that the country rejected during and after the war. He offered the symbolic image of a returning soldier brought back honorably to his nation's proud and loving bosom; in doing this, the President dramatized a reacceptance by the country of those qualities the rhetorical character (i.e., the corpse) symbolized. He held up the unknown hero as a mirror to show us ourselves, but as a mirror on which he had already painted certain features:

This young American understood that freedom is never more than a generation away from extinction. He may not have wanted to be a hero, but there was a need—in the Iron Triangle, off Yankee Station, at Khe Sanh, over the Red River Valley.

He accepted his mission and did his duty.

Listing battlefields spread all over South Vietnam, the President made the Unknown Serviceman ubiquitous; not tied to any one location, the soldier metaphorically represents all who served in Vietnam and, by extension, the entire American culture from which he came including, evidently, all true (i.e., nonprotesting) "young Americans."

Two traits mark Reagan's Unknown and Universal Soldier: unquestioning obedience to the United States government; and a clear understanding of the war, its motives, and its consequences. Personifying this wisdom and duty, the soldier does *not* accurately capture the entire truth of the American experience in Vietnam, among either civilians or the military. An unusually unpopular war (with reservations even on the part of loyal and courageous members of the military), the Vietnam conflict did anything but inspire the kind of consensus and conviction that the President described. Dissent in the field went far beyond mere grumbling. Soldiers organized political study groups, assassinated their own officers, and often returned home to take up leadership in veterans' movements against the war. The notion that the unknown soldier and those whom he typified understood the war is even more far-fetched. Throughout the war and in the years since, this country has wrestled with the disillusionments, doubts, and profound questions raised by the war. Dozens of films, plays, novels, essays, and other explorations have probed and sifted through the war years in search of some meaning. As a fictive creation who stood for not just soldiers, but more for our whole society, the soldier had to understand the war to be ideologically useful. Reagan allowed no room for ambiguity in the hearts of his simplified stock characters. The unknown soldier is, after all, the perfect American hero: "his honest patriotism overwhelms us," said Reagan, putting feelings in our hearts, and belief in our minds; "We understand the meaning of his sacrifice and those of his comrades yet to return." Of course, that meaning is exactly what we do not understand.

The troubles of the past put to rest, the President turned to the future, with special concern for the possibility of another Vietnamese experience. Facing the grim prospect of similar military involvement, Reagan cautioned that we should keep the image of the unknown soldier with us:

This American hero may not need us, but we surely need him. In Longfellow's words:

So when a great man dies,
For years beyond our ken,
The light he leaves behind him lies
Upon the paths of men.

We must not be blind to the light that he left behind. Our path must be worthy of his trust. And we must not betray his love of country.

(The verse comes from Longfellow's "Charles Sumner," a eulogy written in 1874 for the Massachusetts senator who refused to compromise with the South over slavery and preferred war over moral or ideological conciliation. Sumner makes an apt figure to have in the background of Reagan's speech since, during the Civil War, Abraham Lincoln considered him the conscience of the country—a symbolic role quite like that fulfilled by the unknown serviceman.)

Ever since Pericles defended his expansionistic policies by urging the citizens of Athens not to call off his war and cause their sons to have died in vain, leaders have used the death of some soldiers to justify sending others to battle. This appeal begs the question, replacing any original questions about a war's wisdom with the new matter of loyalty not to a president or his policy, but to our lost comrades. After the end of our combat in Vietnam, Americans have proven stubbornly reluctant to become involved overseas militarily. Limited popular support for the 1975 *Mayaguez* incident, the attempted 1980 rescue of American hostages in Iran, and the brief Grenada mission of 1983 have been exceptions in a national attitude that clearly opposes enterprises in Lebanon or in Central America. A President who has a reputation for bellicosity, Ronald Reagan used his faceless hero of the Vietnam War to refute voters' doubts about the use of military force by redirecting our attention as listeners and readers. Using this device, the President turned questioning the Commander-in-Chief and his unelected advisors into blasphemous disrespect for our sanctified dead son. Reagan did not praise the Unknown Serviceman for his physical courage or for battlefield prowess, after all, but for his ardent belief in the American Dream as articulated by the President.

Regardless of the specific sterotype the President might use to make his point, the real heroes of Reagan's American drama are the citizens themselves, the men and women represented by the soldiers, mothers, and other characters we encounter. In the 1981 inaugural address that culminated his long race for the White House, Reagan told Americans that we had to regain the confident optimism that he felt we had lost under Jimmy Carter. "We're too great a nation to limit ourselves to small dreams," he said,

We have every right to dream heroic dreams. Those who say that we're in a time when there are no heroes, they just don't know where to look. . . . I'm addressing the heroes of whom I speak—you, the citizens of this blessed land.

Reagan told Americans to imagine wonderful scenarios for the country, and then told them to make themselves the protagonists of that epic of progress. Such an exhortation of the common American could be construed as a call for realism, curing a sense of inadequacy by dispelling dangerous illusions. Reagan sought just the opposite effect, however, as he told his countrymen to believe in even more splendid visions. Rather than force people to face the constraints of life in our world, Reagan stressed their capabilities. And like many good storytellers, he promised that it could all come true if Americans could only find it in their hearts to believe:

> The crisis we are facing today . . . [requires] our willingness to be-lieve in ourselves and to believe in our capacity to perform great deeds; to believe that together with God's help we can and will resolve the problems which now confront us.
> And, after all, why shouldn't we believe that? We are Americans.

And, once again, Reagan told a joint session of Congress on April 28, 1981 that his economic recovery plan depended most of all on our total faith in it. "[A]ll we need to begin with is a dream that we can do better than before," he said; "All we need to have is faith, and that dream will come true." As the example of the faithful and obedient Unknown Serviceman showed us, Reagan's idealized countrymen are above all a people who believe in them-selves and in their adventure. Belief, not intellect, not skeptical analysis, and not even independent action is the first necessity to fulfill the American Dream according to Ronald Reagan. And this acceptance is more than simply giving the new plan a chance without prejudice: it involves a passionate, almost religious, en-thusiasm. We should expect this demand from one who lives by and in a sense within metaphor.

If unquestioning faith is the characteristic virtue of Reagan's heroes, then intellectual skepticism is the hubristic sin that can bring the world down in ruin. Reagan's villains are intellectuals who presume superiority over the man of common sense because intellectuals, supposedly, assume that they are, to put it plainly, smarter. These include academics, intellectuals, professional lib-eral politicians, and, of course, communists. However, even if it is assumed that people with an active, constantly questioning, and aggressive frame of mind are necessary to address life, nevertheless, the Great Communicator, who employs fictive testimonies of faith to hold his own world together, apparently distrusts such thinking. Like the seemingly well-meaning liberals who corrupt our national souls with too-generous social programs, these cerebral figures threaten to unravel our entire society under the guise of doing us good. Pretending to seek new solutions, they merely make new problems, and would first confuse, then mislead, and finally divide us.

Whether attacking liberals or the Soviet Union, the President pictures all threats to his America as differing from each other only in degree. Reagan presents us with the prospect of choosing between the conclusions arising from an intellectual "evil" or the "truths" of the American heart. Reagan explained the choice in "A Time for Choosing": "Either we accept the responsibility for our own destiny, or we abandon the American Revolution and confess that an intellectual belief in a far-distant capitol can plan our lives for us better than we can plan them ourselves." Always somehow out of touch with *real* America and the world as it actually is, academics and scholars appear in his speeches as sometimes laughable, often dangerous, and always two-dimensional characters.

College professors make especially tempting targets. One of Reagan's first official acts as governor was to respond to the student movements at the University of California's Berkeley campus, an encounter that brought him into direct confrontation with what he saw as an intellectual conspiracy to ruin all that is truly American. In a 1966 speech entitled "The Morality Gap at Berkeley," he blamed the campus turmoil on "a small minority of beatniks, radicals and filthy speech advocates" who were doing their best to turn the school into "a rallying point for Communists and a center of sexual misconduct."[3] The ultimate responsibility, though, lay with the faculty for encouraging this

degeneracy in the guise of scholarship. The first step back to
righteousness, suggested Reagan, would be curbing professors:
"The faculty could also be given a code of conduct that would
force them to serve as examples of good behavior and decency for
the young people in their charge." He demanded "mature, responsible conduct" from the faculty and insisted that they "be
proponents of those ethical and moral standards demanded by the
great majority of our society." The cause of the problems was the
very refusal by the teachers to impose this Reaganist code of
"family values" on their young charges:

> What in Heaven's name does academic freedom have to do with
> rioting, with anarchy, with attempts to destroy the primary purpose of
> the University which is to educate our young people?
> When those who advocate an open mind keep it open at both ends
> with no thought process in the middle, the open mind becomes a hose
> for any idea that comes along. If scholars are to be recognized as having
> a right to press their particular value judgements, perhaps the time has
> come also for institutions of higher learning to assert themselves as
> positive forces in the battle for men's minds.

Reagan's vilification of the Berkeley faculty exemplifies perfectly
how he usually portrays intellectuals.

The word *education* comes from the Latin words *ex* and *duco*,
meaning respectively "out of" and "to lead"; to educate someone,
especially in the liberal arts, is to lead them out of one condition
into another. It is ideally a process of liberation in which a student gains freedom and power to undertake his or her own explorations. If education is "a battle for men's [and women's] minds,"
it is so in the truest sense only when those minds end up not
possessed by their teachers, but free and able to decide—or not to
decide—on their own authority. But according to Reagan's fond
and didactic memories of his own school days, schools should be
temples not of intellectual freedom, but of traditional morality
and values in concert with "common sense." Public school

teachers, who act as surrogate parents for our young children, rank high on the President's list of heroes. Reminiscing on his 73rd birthday with deceptive fondness about the hard times of his childhood, Reagan praised good elementary teachers for their work on behalf of American confidence. "Dixon held together," he said, "Our faith was our strength. Our teachers pointed to the future."

In 1967, at the height of campus protests against the Vietnam War, Reagan dedicated a new library at Eureka College. In his speech he reduced the rigorous challenges of a college education to a loyal reliance on the wisdom of the past. He sent students to their new library in search of Aristotle, Plato, and Socrates, and offered the Bible as the single most crucial holding in Eureka's collection. "Can you name one problem that would not be solved," he asked, "if we had simply followed the teachings of the man from Galilee?"

A good teacher preaches the "family values" of piety and patriotism; the greatest teacher of all is Jesus. In his eagerness to blame student discord not on real issues but on an easily identified foe, Reagan often singles out academics as the source of society's woes. In his 1970 speech, "Ours is Not a Sick Society," he scorned intellectuals who pick on the American establishment. "[T]his has been compounded by the accusations of our sons and daughters who pride themselves on 'telling it like it is,'" he explained. Reagan blamed the falsehoods on universities: "Well, I have news for them—in a thousand social science courses, they have been taught 'the way it is *not*.'" Again in 1973, in a speech called "Why the Conservative Movement is Growing," he complained, "Our sons and daughters, in too many social science courses, are taught the same fairy tale" about liberalism's benefits and imagined emergencies requiring federal intention; "Little men with loud voices cry doom, seeing little that is good in America. They create fear and uncertainty among us." And in his Bicentennial television address of July, 1976, he declared that the American people had never "fallen for the line of a few fashionable intellectuals and academics who in recent years would have us believe ours is a sick society—a bad country."

Anti-intellectualism has a long tradition in America, and Ronald Reagan has quite comfortably made it part of his fictive persona. There are some biographical reasons that might account for his attitude, such as the proverbial small-town distrust of "new-fangled ideas" and his oft-confessed lack of interest in making any more effort in college than was required to maintain his eligibility for football. Yet we would be as wrong to accept this self-characterization as the true one as we would to believe in Reagan's other personae. Reagan is no more purely this character than he is the Gipper, no matter how hard he tries to convince us. While living in Hollywood (hardly a hotbed of intellectual fervor) Reagan actually had something of a reputation as a ponderous man of ideas. Jane Wyman seems to have divorced him, at least in part, because she found his intellectual interests and zeal too profound for the kind of life she wanted. It was exasperating, she told a friend, "to have someone at the breakfast table, newspaper in hand, expounding on the far right, far left, conservative right, the conservative left, the middle of the road."[4] Reagan's liberal opponents might like to think of him as a dunderhead with no ideas, but in so doing they misunderstand the President and his conservative followers.

Despite the populist strain of its rhetoric, the revitalized Republican party that put Mr. Reagan into the White House is beyond any doubt an intellectually active coalition. Retooling the organization in preparation for the campaign of 1980, Reagan and his conservative brain trust changed the GOP from within by infusing it with highly theoretical ideas about defense, religion, the Constitution, and supply-side economics. Universities have, in fact, been the source of many of Reagan's policies, as have high-power conservative think tanks such as the American Enterprise Institute, the Hoover Institute, and the Heritage Foundation. Reagan usually plays down the intellectual character of his coalition, though, being careful to present it as plain common sense originating in the hearts of the voters.

One thing that must be made clear in post-Watergate is this: the American new conservative majority we represent is *not* based on abstract theorizing of the kind that turns off the American people, but on common sense, intelligence, reason, hard work, faith in God, and the guts to say, yes, there *are* things we do strongly believe in, that we are willing to live for, and, yes, if necessary to die for. This is not "ideological purity." It is simply what built this country and kept it great.

Let us lay to rest, once and for all, the myth of a small group of ideological purists trying to capture a majority. Replace it with the reality of a majority trying to assert its rights against the tyranny of powerful academics, fashionable left-revolutionaries, some economic illiterates who happen to hold elective office, and the social engineers who dominate the dialogue and set the format in political and social affairs. If there is any ideological fanaticism in American political life, it is to be found among the enemies of freedom on the left and right— those who would sacrifice principle to theory, those who would worship only the god of political, social, and economic abstractions, ignoring the realities of everyday life. They are *not* conservatives.

"Conservatism is the antithesis of the kind of ideological fanaticism that has brought so much horror and destruction to the world," explained Reagan, "The common sense and common decency of ordinary men and women, working out their own lives in their own way—this is the heart of American conservatism today." Reagan's conservative theory specifically does not "turn off the American people." In a fictive world painted in black and white, foolish academics who keep insisting on grey will never prevail. Conservative Americans temper their ratiocination with "faith in God"; liberal intellectuals apostatize themselves and would sacrifice morality on the altar of intellect. By juxtaposing the left and right in these terms, Ronald Reagan gives what should be purely political differences the aura of a moral contest between devout common-sense patriots and God-less ideologues.

Although the sincerity and thoroughness of his position has come under question, Ronald Reagan has always presented him-self as an antigovernment candidate who champions the simple aspirations and solutions sought by real Americans. "In this pres-ent crisis, government is not the solution to our problem," he said in his 1981 inaugural address, "government is the problem." And the worst flaw with the federal establishment is that it resem-bles all too closely the academic communities that Reagan blasted as governor of California. Tenure allows professors intellectual freedom that Reagan considers moral license; bureaucrats have a kind of institutional tenure as well. Firing a civil servant is no easy task, and the schemes of the federal bureaucracy resemble the self-gratifying projects of academia in their inspiration, their removal from the "real world," and in their invulnerability to attack. The President has many times joked that the nearest thing to an immortal creation on earth is a federal program. Liberal bureaucrats also appear in Reagan's stories as quasi-intellectual schemers, "an array of planners, grantsmen, and professional middlemen" like the obsessive thoughtful bureaucrats who wrote the 250 feet of construction regulations or who somehow saw an abstract wisdom in initialing erased initials. Whenever the so-called "idea men" get involved in a project and work against the natural wisdom of the American heart, implies the President, failure surely follows. Calling for an end to federal studies and the implementation of simpler measures to curb crime, Reagan told the International Association of Chiefs of Police in 1981, "It's time, too, that we acknowledge the solution to the crime problem will not be found in the social worker's files, the psychiatrist's notes, or the bureaucrats' budgets. It's a problem of the human heart, and it's there we must look for the answer."

Excessive paperwork is not the most serious threat posed by the intellect. The danger of too much thinking and not enough believing is that the chimeric creations of academia will come alive. Liberals are intellectuals who have somehow wormed their way into the government. When left unchecked, they can lead, in the President's world picture, to a terrifying statist extreme. However, the danger of the schemes and theories of social workers and federal planners shrink when compared to the really awesome dangers of that grandest intellectual invention, communism. Karl Marx, after all, wrote *Das Kapital* in the reading room of the British Museum, a veritable inner sanctum of scholars.[5] The grand crusade of the twentieth century is, in the words of President Reagan, a contest between the faithful heart and the poisonously clever intellect. At he explained in his 1982 "New Year's Remarks to Foreign Peoples."

During my lifetime, I have seen the rise of fascism and communism. Both philosophies glorify the arbitrary power of the state. These ideologies held, at first, a certain fascination for some intellectuals. But both theories fail. Both deny those God-given liberties that are the inalienable right of each person on this planet; indeed they deny the existence of God. Because of this fundamental flaw, fascism has already been destroyed, and the bankruptcy of communism has been laid bare for all to see—a system that is efficient in producing machines of war but cannot feed its people.

Communism began as an idea that took shape by possessing the minds of men and women and then slowly destroyed their souls. Stripped of the wisdom of the heart's own faith, too many men and women of the twentieth century have become automatons in service to theory. Lacking all humanity, the godless communist state emerges in Reagan's rhetoric as a mechanistic opposite to the symbol of the pure and faithful American heart. Reagan put his conviction graphically in his 1977 "Reshaping the American Political Landscape."

Only now and then do we in the West hear a voice from out of that darkness. Then there is silence—the silence of human slavery. There is no more terrifying sound in human experience, with one possible exception. Look at that map [on which communist countries were shaded in black] again. The very heart of the darkness is the Soviet Union and from that heart comes a different sound. It is the whirling sound of machinery and the whisper of the computer technology we ourselves have sold them. It is the sound of building, building of the strongest military machine ever devised by man.

The American heart and its pious virtues are the center of Reagan's heroism. Mothers are "the heart of the family," and the Iowa farms comprise "the heartland" from which flow truth and goodness. But under the intellectual influence of Karl Marx, the arch-social scientist, the human heart dies beneath the wheels of an ideological juggernaut.

The dramatic tension in Reagan's epic narrative resolves into a "battle for men's minds," fought not so much with guns and bombs as with symbols, language, and propaganda. As the President said in his speech of July 19, 1982 marking Captive Nations Week, "Two visions of the world remain locked in dispute." When using rhetoric to defend his American vision, Mr. Reagan wages war with imagery that conjures up sublime and terrible scenes, transforming the physical world into an allegorical battleground between good and evil. The farms of Iowa or the hearths of American homes are the sources of good just as the Soviet Union is the "heart of the darkness." That is, the farms of the America "heartland" are the locus of virtue, the symbolic opposite of the Kremlin. Likewise, the divided city of Berlin, where the wall separates Reagan's world, is the most symbolically charged setting in Reagan's war between heart and intellect.

The meeting place of East and West, split by the grim wall, the former capitol of Germany has long been a striking emblem of the confrontation of democracy and communism. When John Kennedy visited the city and declared, *"Ich bin ein Berliner,"* he captured the poetic meaning of Berlin for the western allies as the frontier outpost of freedom in its "long twilight struggle" against totalitarianism. "To be a Berliner," Reagan has added, "is to live the great historic struggle of this age, the latest chapter in man's timeless quest for freedom." The President put his vision of Berlin quite poetically in a 1982 address delivered outside the Charlottenburg Palace, only a short walk from the wall. An emotional pastiche of imagery and motifs, the speech has striking sense of myth and metaphor from its first paragraph on:

It was one of Germany's greatest sons, Goethe, who said that "there is strong shadow where there is much light." In our time Berlin, more than any other place in the world, is such a meeting place of light and shadow, tyranny and freedom. To be here is truly to stand on freedom's edge and in the shadow of a wall that has come to symbolize all that is darkest in the world today, to sense how shining and priceless and how much in need of constant vigilance and protection our legacy of liberty is.

Berlin, said the President, "is more than a place on a map—[it is] a city that is a testament to what is both most inspiring and most troubling about the time we live in."

The bulk of Reagan's address consists of the history of Soviet deeds in recent years and of an appeal for new initiatives between the USSR and the USA. He rehearsed a series of Russian crimes— the occupation of Afghanistan, the suppression of Poland's Solidarity union, stationing missiles in East Germany, and violations of the Helsinki accord on human rights—then pleaded with Soviet leader Leonid Brezhnev to take steps towards new liberalization in order "to fulfill the promise that [the 1972 Berlin Quadripartite Agreement] seemed to offer at its dawn." His case made, the President ended the speech by talking about the role of the people of Berlin in East-West relations. Reagan's message pitted the image of the wall against the soul of freedom:

Yes, the hated wall still stands. But taller and stronger than that bleak barrier dividing East from West, free from oppressed, stands the character of the Berliners themselves. You have endured in your splendid city on the Spree, and my return visit has convinced me, in the words of the beloved old song that "Berline bleibt doch Berlin."—Berlin is still Berlin.

We all remember John Kennedy's stirring words when he visited Berlin. I can only add that we in America and in the West are still Berliners, too, and always will be. And I am proud to say today that it is good to be home again.

In this symbolic place and moment, the heart alone, as expressed by Reagan in his depiction of a united, faithful, determined West under American leadership, has the power to assault the concrete fortress of mechanized, hyperintellectualized Marxist ideology.

NOTES

1. M. H. Abrams, *A Glossary of Literary Terms*, 4th edition, (New York: Holt, Rinehart and Winston, 1981), p. 20.
2. Reagan and Hubler, *Where's the Rest of Me?* (New York: Duell, Sloan and Pearce, 1965), pp. 13, 18.
3. Ronald Reagan, "The Morality Gap at Berkeley," in *The Creative Society* (New York: Devin-Adair, 1968), pp. 125–27.
4. Cannon, p. 64; citing Robert Perrella, *They Call Me the Showbiz Priest* (New York: Trident Press, 1973), no page number given.
5. While preparing this manuscript, I came upon an amusingly apt quotation from Mikhail Gorbachev's December 1984 trip to London: "If people don't like Marxism, they should blame the British Museum." *The New York Times*, March 12, 1985, p. A–16.

5 / AMERICA'S DIVINE DESTINY

Reagan translates the relatively mundane details of political life into a variety of new narrative contexts. He reduces questions about economic planning, constitutional interpretation, national defense, and all other matters to their most basic emotional level and presents them as parts of a struggle between good and evil. The ideological and territorial conflict of the United States and the Soviet Union functions as one such dramatization. An even grander frame of reference, though, subsumes all of Reagan's many stories and myths—Christianity. Many times Reagan has explained the cosmological implications of the various oppositions in the East-West debate according to this spiritual vision. Communism and fascism are doomed, he has said, because of a single fundamental flaw: "They deny the existence of God." The conflict between America and the Soviet Union over political principles belongs to a larger struggle, the eternal war between God and Satan.

To the great delight of politicized born-again Christian organizations and to the distress of civil libertarians, Ronald Reagan has made this country's spiritual renewal a key goal of his administration. Despite the fact that he does not attend church regularly, or hold regular White House prayer meetings in the manner of Richard Nixon, President Reagan emphasizes religion in his public rhetoric and ceremonial appearances. As Governor of California he instituted regular prayer breakfasts, a custom retained in the White House. It was at one of these meetings, in fact, that Reagan announced that whatever time remained for him after surviving an assassination attempt belongs to God. Recalling his pledge to restore Americans' belief in themselves, Reagan told the American Conservative Union in 1977, "Our cause must be to rediscover, reassert, and reapply America's spiritual heritage to our national affairs." During the campaign of 1980, he went to considerable lengths to woo conservative religious backers such as Jerry Falwell and the Moral Majority. Introduced by evangelist James Robertson to over 17,000 ardent Christians in Dallas, the future President blasted his liberal opponents as apostates. "Over the last two or three decades, the federal government seems to have forgotten that old-time religion and that old-time Constitution," he said; "It's time for God's people to come out of the closet. Religious America is awakening, perhaps just in time for the country's sake."[1] It is curious to note that even though Jimmy Carter and John Anderson—and not Ronald Reagan—were avowed born-again Christians, only Reagan accepted the invitation to speak in Dallas.

Since taking office, Reagan has kept up his connections with the Christian right. He has regularly addressed the National Religious Broadcasters Association and the National Association of Evangelicals. On March 19, 1981, the President proclaimed a National Day of Prayer and expressed his wish that "more of our citizens would, through prayer, come into a closer relationship with their Maker." The President told the National Religious Broadcasters in 1982 that he saw something great happpening in America. "I have always believed," he said, "that this country— not always, but in recent years, I should say, believed that this country is hungering for a spiritual revival." Responding to liberal complaints that fundamentalists imposed their views on others, the President underlined his conviction that America could not survive without their faith:

If we have come to the point in America where any attempt to see traditional values reflected in public policy would leave one open to irresponsible charges, then I say the entire structure of our free society is threatened. . . . It's time to realize, I think, that we need God more than he needs us.

Proclaiming a National Day of Prayer in 1982, President Reagan echoed Christ's promise to Peter that he would be the rock upon which the Christian church would rise. "Together," preached Reagan, "let us take up the challenge to reawaken America's religious and moral heart, recognizing that a deep and abiding faith in God is the rock upon which this great nation was founded." The truest American heart belongs to God and country.

Lest America fail to follow its Christian duty, Reagan occasionally reminds listeners of the risks they run if they do not fulfill the responsibility. Endorsing Jesse Helms (whose long year of battling for "family values" Reagan compares to David's fight with Goliath) in 1983, the President offered the paradigmatic Judeo-Christian alternatives, destruction or glory:

We Americans are blessed in so many ways. We're a nation under God, a living and loving God. But Thomas Jefferson warned us, "I tremble for my country when I reflect that God is just." We cannot expect Him to protect us in a crisis if we turn away from Him in our every day living. But you know, He told us what to do in II Chronicles. Let us reach out to Him. He said, "If my people, which are called by my name, shall humble themselves and pray and seek my face and turn from their wicked ways, then will I hear from Heaven and will forgive their sin and will heal their land."

"I recognize we must be cautious in claiming that God is on our side," President Reagan said in the 1984 State of the Union Address that barely preceded his announcement to seek reelection, "but I think it's all right to keep asking if we're on His side."

We should realize when considering President Reagan's use of religious language that his posture is decidedly Christian, even though he often speaks of "the Judeo-Christian tradition." When Reagan speaks of the Jewish faith in America, he does so in a manner seemingly suggestive that Judaism is a superfluous and perhaps even a false faith in America. Apart from speeches to specifically Jewish organizations (which he makes rarely), Reagan mentions exclusively Judaic beliefs only in the context of Christianity. Wishing the nation a merry Christmas on December 23, 1981, the President spoke of two icons visible from his residence:

Just across the way from from the White House stand the two great symbols of the holiday season: a Menorah, symbolizing the Jewish festival of Hanukkah, and the National Christmas Tree, a beautiful towering blue spruce from Pennsylvania. Like the National Christmas Tree, our country is a living, growing thing.

At first reading, the passage above appears altogether ecumenical—at least in regard to Christians and Jews if not to members of other faiths or to atheists. However, a subtle discrimination marks the President's comments. The Menorah symbolizes only Judaism; the National Christmas Tree represents all of America. That Reagan was speaking, after all, on a Christian holiday might excuse the apparent slight that he gave Jews. Yet, the same undercurrents run through speeches Reagan has delivered on Jewish holy days. Delivering a radio address entitled "Prayer" to the nation on Rosh Hashanah (the first day of the Hebrew calendar), 1982, the President noted the holiday and said, "So, to all of our friends and neighbors observing this holiday—and speaking for all Americans—I want to wish a happy, peaceful, and prosperous New Year." As he did in the Christmas message, Mr. Reagan sounded altogether cordial, but he still gave unmistakeable signals that even though the elected leader of a society in which church and state are constitutionally separated, he speaks for the national Christian community. The phrase "all of our friends and neighbors" sets American Jews apart from the "us" implied by "our." Further, when the President spoke "for all Americans" to the Jews, seemingly as though they comprised a distinct community, he articulated a Christian point of view. "I know there are those who recognize Christmas Day as the birthday of a great and good man, a wise teacher who gave us principles to live by," he said of Jews in 1982, "And then there are those of us who believe that he was the Son of God, that he was divine." Defending his school prayer amendment to the United States Consitution, the President used language that seems almost calculated to make non-Christians uncomfortable. "Our only hope for tomorrow is in the faces of our children," he said in 1983, "And we know Jesus said, 'Suffer the little children to come unto me, and forbid them not, for such is the Kingdom of God.'"

The *locus classicus* of Reagan's vision of a Christian America is his 1983 speech to the National Association of Evangelicals in Orlando, Florida. One of his most controversial addresses, the speech triggered an international uproar by translating domestic and foreign policy debates into an apocalyptic Christian parable. It provides a superb example of how the President aims for communion with his listeners in a preacherly as well as a political sense, and of how he applies the interpretations of his public Christianity to matters that might seem to some unconnected.

Reagan began the Orlando speech with some typical anecdotes. One illustrated his belief in intercessionary prayer with the story of how he once told a congressman who was going to seek divine intervention on behalf on legislation that "if sometimes when he was praying he got a busy signal, it was just me in there ahead of him." Another mocked the morality of politicians (to whose profession Reagan claims steadfastly not to belong) by depicting the warm welcome a politician received in Heaven. Curious why he should have a grand mansion filled with servants while clergymen lived in small huts, the new arrival learned that he was the first of his kind ever let through the Pearly Gates. The President quickly drew a distinction, of course, between himself and his conservative allies in government and the average (and presumably liberal) politician: "I'll tell you there are a great many God-fearing, dedicated, noble men and women in public life, present company included." Celebrating the "great spiritual awakening" that he saw in America, he vowed that the items on the Association's program "must be a key part of the Nation's political agenda."

Reagan spoke of school prayer, abortion, and the proposed "squeal rule" to require health clinics to inform parents when their under-age daughters seek birth control advice. As the speech progressed, though, he addressed a far more reaching concern: the spirit of "modern-day secularism" which denies the premises of evangelical Christianity. Liberals, he warned in a typical passage, "proclaim that they're freeing us from superstitions of the past" only in order to discard "the tried and time-tested values upon which our very civilization is based." We have seen how Reagan portrays liberal intellectuals in the moral battles of this world. Speaking to the evangelists in a religious context, the President linked political liberalism with "secular humanism." (The term *humanist* has had many meanings over the centuries—some of them quite contrary to the current popular definition; in the Renaissance, Christian humanism was a very strong religious movement. When used by fundamental conservative Christian groups, the word now means "atheist.") Reagan used this connection to move into the main body of his address, which

77

he began by reminding his listeners of the dangers and limits of the human intellect and of the folly of liberalism:

> Now obviously, much of this new political and social consensus I've talked about is based on a positive view of American history, one that takes pride in our country's accomplishments and record. But we must never forget that no government schemes are going to perfect man. We know that living in this world means dealing with what philosophers would call the phenomenology of evil or, as theologians would put it, the docrine of sin. There is evil and sin in the world, and we're enjoined by Scripture and the Lord Jesus to oppose it with all our might.

With humility apparently appropriate for one speaking from the pulpit, Reagan granted that his people had erred from time to time in the past, but he insisted that "any objective observer must hold a positive view of American history, a history that has been the story of hopes fulfilled and dreams made into reality." The true source of evil in the world is the Soviet Union. While the United States has "in this century . . . kept alight the torch of freedom," the Russians "have openly and publicly declared that the only morality they recognize is that which will further their cause, which is world revolution." Recalling his disgust at the liberals who blasphemously sought to free humanity from "superstitions," Reagan quoted Lenin's denunciation of all morality that proceeds from "supernatural ideas"—"their [i.e., the Soviets'] name for religion."

Reagan told one of his favorite stories to show the zeal with which God-fearing Americans ought to resist Marxist docrines. It is the tale of a good American family:

> A number of years ago, I heard a young father, a very prominent young man in the entertainment world [i.e., Pat Boone], addressing a tremendous gathering in California. It was during the time of the cold war, and communism and our own way of life were very much on people's minds. And he was speaking to that subject. And suddenly, though, I heard him saying, "I love my little girls more than anything—"

And I said to myself, "Oh, no don't. You can't—don't say that." But I had underestimated him. He went on: "I would rather see my little girls die now, still believing in God, then have them grow up under communism and one day die no longer believing in God.

The audience of "thousands of young people," reported Reagan, "came to their feet with shouts of joy."

The anecdote reveals the depth of President Reagan's fear of Marxism. To him the Soviet system threatens not only our way of life on earth, but also the fate of our immortal souls. And communism threatens to do more than strip us of our faith. Soviets are, according to this speech, an active, organized force working deliberately to undo God's work. "[L]et us pray for the salvation of all of those who live in that totalitarian darkness—pray they will discover the joy of knowing God," said the President;

But until they do, let us be aware that while they preach the supremacy of the state, declare its omnipotence over individual man, and predict its eventual domination of all peoples on the Earth, they are the focus of evil in the modern world.

The word "might" had a specific meaning in the address quoted above—nuclear weapons. Among the subjects to be discussed by those attending the Orlando convention was the proposed nuclear freeze resolution. Like the "foot in the door" schemes of liberals, the freeze represents for Reagan an insidious communist scheme to weaken and divide America. Granting that his administration would seek an understanding with the USSR, he vowed nonetheless, "we will never compromise our principles and standards . . . never abandon our belief in God." He denounced the freeze movement as "a very dangerous fraud" and called it an "illusion of peace." Knowing that the freeze had adherents among the evangelicals, President Reagan linked its ultimate supporters with the Anti-Christ, the false messiah who will delude the faithful. He quoted C. S. Lewis' *Screwtape Letters*, a collection of essays in the from of letters from a senior devil to a junior imp. "The greatest evil," wrote Lewis, ". . . is conceived and ordered (moved, seconded, carried and minuted) in clear, carpeted, warmed, and well-lighted offices, by quiet men with white collars and cut fingernails and smooth-shaven cheeks who do not need to raise their voice." Reagan warned that because these earthly devils seem so pleasant, "because they sometimes speak in soothing tones of brotherhood and peace," well-meaning Americans are seduced by their mellifluous promises.

So in your discussions of the nuclear freeze proposals, I urge you to beware the temptation of pride—the temptation of blithely declaring yourselves above it all and label both sides equally at fault, to ignore the facts of history and the aggressive impulses of an evil empire, to simply call the arms race a giant misunderstanding and thereby remove yourself from the struggle between right and wrong and good and evil.

To make his point more forcefully, President Reagan evoked Whittaker Chambers, who, he said, proved that "the crisis of the Western World exists to the degree in which the West is indifferent to God, the degree to which it collaborates in communism's attempt to make man stand alone without God. . . . Marxism-Leninism is actually the second oldest faith, first proclaimed in the Garden of Eden with the words of temptation, "Ye shall be as gods."

Whittaker Chambers, the "tragic and lonely" man to whom Reagan compared himself in the closing days of his tours for General Electric, differs from most of Reagan's characters in that he has a name and a detailed biography. Once a member of the Communist party and confessedly active in an espionage operation aimed at the United States government, Chambers instigated a national uproar when, in 1948, he accused Alger Hiss, a highly placed State Department official in the Roosevelt administration, of having spied for the Soviets. Alger Hiss testified under oath to the House Un-American Affairs Committee that he had never even met Chambers. Hiss was accused of perjuring himself and tried. The perjury trial divided the nation and seemed a moral test of America in the early years of the cold war. As an aftermath, Chambers became a symbol of loyalty to those who believe in Hiss's guilt. To others, who do not believe that Hiss lied, Chamber symbolizes the expression of right-wing paranoia. Controversial as Whittaker Chambers may seem to many Americans, President Reagan sees him as perhaps the wisest man of our century. As he said to the ostensibly non-religious Conservative Political Action Conference in 1981,

> The crisis of the Western world, Whittaker Chambers reminded us, exists to the degree in which it is indifferent to God. "The Western world does not know it," he said about our struggle, "but it already possesses the answer to this problem—but only provided that its faith in God and the freedom He enjoins is as great as Communism's faith in man."

President Reagan has described Chambers in glowing language, using words normally applied to literary characters. Posthumously awarding Chambers the Medal of Freedom in March, 1984, Reagan said the trial "symbolized our century's epic struggle between freedom and totalitarianism." "The solitary figure of Whittaker Chambers," he maintained, "personified the mystery of human redemption in the face of evil and suffering."

Reagan's admiration for Chambers has puzzled many analysts. Most concur that the President sees a parallel between his own disaffection from the Democratic party in the 1950s and Chambers' decision to leave the communists. This interpretation makes a good deal of sense, but we can understand Chambers' meaning for the President better if we look at how Reagan uses him in his speeches. In the repertoire of Reagan's symbolic characters, Whittaker Chambers stands as the allegorical champion of the free world and the prophet of a Christian conservative victory over "the second oldest faith, first proclaimed [by Satan] in the

Garden of Eden": liberalism and communism. Chambers' conversion from communism was a miniature of the spiritual revolution that Reagan sees in America. Strikingly, he first broke with
his comrades over abortion. No professional revolutionary, he
believed, could have children. Yet when he discovered that his
wife had become pregnant and began to contemplate doing away
with the fetus, Chambers experienced a moment of rebirth. "A
wild joy swept me," he wrote in *Witness*, ". . . the Communist
Party and its theories . . . crumbled at the touch of a child."
Reagan told the story of the final break in his 1982 Conservative
Political Action Conference address:

> Whittaker Chambers . . . wrote very movingly of his moment of
> awakening. It was at breakfast, and he was looking at the delicate ear of
> his tiny baby daughter, and he said that, suddenly, looking at that, he
> knew that couldn't just be an accident of nature. He said, while he
> didn't realize it at the time, he knows now that in that moment God had
> touched his forehead with his finger.

Whittaker Chambers is the quintessential hero of Reagan's
crusade to make the United States a nation firmly under God.
Lured by big government in its most extreme form, pulled towards
atheism and nearly persuaded to abort his own child, Chambers
typologically exemplifies the American people in Reagan's gospel. He enunciated the spiritual and political creed that Ronald
Reagan has held for 30 years, and his conversion from communism in a flash of Christian revelation epitomizes the very fusion
of politics and belief that characterizes Reagan's sermons. Chambers quite explicitly underwent an ecstatic rebirth, regenerating
from faith in the state to a Christian belief in the virtues of family
and American conservative patriotism. We see in the parable of
Chambers just how closely Reagan identifies the renewal of patriotism with the religious revival that has inspired so many of his
political supporters.

The sense of confrontation between the United States and the

Soviets as armies respectively of God and Satan points to a religious motif that runs throughout Reagan's epic of America: the
theme of Armageddon. The notion that our world will eventually
fulfill its destiny in some cataclysmic fight between cosmic good
and evil has many expressions in humanity's various religions and
myths, the most potent of which in Western civilization, stems
from the New Testament revelation of St. John the Divine. According to that book, the symbolic and literalist interpretations of
which have fed many theological and textual debates, the final
battle will take place on the fields of Armageddon. With the
breaking of the last seal, nature will go wild; after terrible earth-
quakes, thunder and lightning storms, and hailstones the likes of
which have never fallen, the heavenly host will arrive:

And I saw heaven opened and beheld a white horse; and he that sat
upon him was faithful and true, and in righteousness he doth judge and
make war. His eyes were as a flame of fire, and on his head were many
crowns. . . . And he was clothed with a vesture dipped in blood, and
his name was called The Word of God. . . . And out of his mouth
goeth a sharp sword, that with it he should smite the nations, and he
shall rule them with a rod of iron, and he treadeth the winepress of the
fierceness and wrath of Almighty God.

The battle follows, in which God's forces overthrow the minions
of the devil and his false prophet, the Anti-Christ:

And the beast was taken, and with him the false prophet . . . and
them that worshipped his image. These were cast alive into a lake of fire
burning with brimstone. And the remnant were slain with the sword of
him that sat upon the horse, which sword proceded out of his mouth:
and all the fowls were filled with their flesh.

The battle concluded, there follow the act of judgment and the
establishment of the New Jerusalem on earth to serve as Christ's
seat for this thousand-year rule. After that ten-century interval
(according to the millenarian or chiliastic tradition), God will

free Satan, then destroy him and his legions entirely before a general resurrection of all dead humans. Obviously, the Book of St. John has received many diverse interpretations since its composition. It may well be that this passage was meant as metaphor. The rider's name and that his weapon is a sword from his mouth might suggest that we should read the scene as a comment on the power of language. (The spoken if not penned word is mightier than the sword, seems to be the lesson.) But this metaphoric interpretation is not popular among the fundamentalists who heed Reagan's religious speeches most deeply.

The closest thing to a standard doctrine of Armageddon among the religious right in America today holds that the world is now under the control of Satan. Basing their belief on a multitude of what they consider reliably decoded signs in the Bible and in the world, many members of Reagan's born-again audiences adhere to the view that in the near future armies of the USSR, Europe, Iran, Arabia, Africa, and China will invade and destroy Israel. All of those armies will perish, most likely as the result of nuclear explosions. A small number of Israelis will survive and convert to Christianity, signaling the "rapture"—a singular phenomenon in which true Christians will rise bodily from the earth to join Christ, who will be encountered riding his white horse. Led by the Messiah, the faithful will defeat Satan in the battle of Armageddon, the details of which resemble those prophesied by St. John the Divine. Nonbelievers may find this scenario altogether unlikely, yet it forms the basis of the religious and political right's expectations for the future. Indeed, the most obvious difference between the biblical and modern fundamental vision of the final battle is that the more recent of the two specifically reflects conservative American political attitudes. (It also helps explain why many fundamental Christians support aid for Israel. The Jewish homeland must exist as a kind of apocalyptic tripwire.)[2]

President Reagan's views on Armageddon are problematic. Given brief but significant attention during the election campaign of 1984, they appear both serious and tentative. He has on a number of occasions spoken about a final cataclysm. Running for president in 1980, candidate Reagan appeared with evangelist Jim Bakker on the PTL (i.e., "Praise the Lord") television network and in discussing his belief that Americans need spiritual renewal, cautioned, "We may be the generation that sees Armageddon." He reportedly told a group of Jewish leaders during the same race, "Israel is the only stable democracy we can rely on in a spot where Armageddon could come." After his inauguration, the President talked about biblical Armageddon with Senator Howard Heflin of Alabama, and said, "Russia is going to get involved in it." The matter received its most public attention in the second debate between President Reagan and Walter Mondale. Asked to explain his position on Armageddon in light of his several remarks, Reagan responded:

I think what has been hailed as something I'm supposedly, as President, discussing as principle is the result of just some philosophical discussions with people who are interested in the same things. And that is the prophecies down through the years, the biblical prophecies of what would portend the coming of Armageddon and so forth. And the fact that a number of theologians for the last decade or more have believed that this was true, that the prophecies are coming together that portend that.

But no one knows whether Armageddon—those prophecies—mean that Armageddon is a thousand years away or the day after tomorrow. So I have never seriously warned and said we must plan according to Armageddon.

Quite properly, the charge that Ronald Reagan believes fervently in the fundamental vision of today's world affairs as apocalypse disappeared almost at once. The President seems at some level to believe in some version of the Armageddon prophecy, but even his most ardent opponents would be hard pressed to prove that Reagan follows the hardline principles of the religious right in their most extreme—and dangerous—expression.

85

For our purposes, the question of whether or not Reagan actually believes in a literal and swiftly approaching final cataclysm is as irrelevant as whether or not he was really in the ball park from which he seemed to be broadcasting for WHO. What does matter, though, are the ways in which he uses the language of Armageddon to create an atmosphere of crisis. Like his other religious remarks, Reagan's talk of biblical prophecies earns him valuable favor among fundamentalists, persons who presumably want someone who shares their belief in power. Reagan applies apocalyptic rhetoric to many other, apparently nonreligious matters. The sense of absolute urgency implied by such talk is a powerful motivator. As early as "A Time for Choosing"—as the very name of that speech suggests—Reagan has presented Americans with prospects of the end of the world, be that end "a thousand years of darkness" under Satanic Marxist rule, or nuclear war brought on by weak American defenses. By speaking (even if only by innuendo and subliminal allusion) of the battle of Armageddon, President Reagan can borrow for any issue the emotional and quasi-spiritual aura of this ancient and entrenched motif. Casting himself as a prophet with one foot in politics and the other in theology, as the elected President of the United States, and as the annointed and protected agent of God, Ronald Reagan becomes a hero of biblical proportions. Members of the religious right may vote for him because they hear in his half-voiced "musings" on Armageddon a confirmation of their own geopolitical theology; even nonbelievers, though, may find themselves responding to the archetypal myth of the end of the world.

In his narrative persona of America's prophet, Reagan offers a double vision of the future. On one hand, he warns that our actions could lead to destruction, but at the same time he promises us glory and success—a thousand years of light—if we hold true to his political vision. This conception of our national future as one of possibilities and choice and not simply of fate (and here, if the point needs making, we see Reagan clearly breaking with the more ardent members of the religious right) is as old as the country itself. Looking back to the Puritans of New England, those men and women whose millenarian religious expectations have shaped our national consciousness, we find that Reagan's prophetic oratory belongs to the genre of the jeremiad. This form dominates American oratory and—some critics would argue—all American literature. Its model is the Old Testament Book of Jeremiah. "Thine own wickedness shall correct thee, and thy backslidings shall reprove thee," spoke the prophet, "know therefore and see that it is an evil thing and bitter, that thou hast forsaken the Lord thy God" (Jeremiah 2:19). Jeremiah lived during the collapse of the kingdom of Judah; he called on the Jews to abandon their new, apostate ways and to obey the laws that God had given to their fathers. A lone voice of conservative orthodoxy in his nation, the prophet created powerful apocalyptic visions and blasted the Jews for backsliding. (We can see in Jeremiah an original for Reagan's Whittaker Chambers and for the President himself when he speaks in the prophetic mode.) The jeremiad form provides a structure for history, and implicit in that structure is profound moral significance and responsibility. It is a medium by which any number of causes can be discussed. (See p. 88–89 for a discussion of an "American" usage of the term "jeremiad.")

The Puritan colonists who came to New England in the 1630s believed that God had elected them as His new chosen people. They were to build in North America the New Jerusalem of the Book of Revelations. God had a scheme for humanity, a plan that was drawn up before Creation and that preordained the progress of the world from Adam and Eve's fall, to the sacrifice of Christ and to the Second Coming and beyond. Convinced that the era described in Revelations drew near, the colonists came to the New World to prepare for the New Age. The sense of mission both inspired and weighed heavily on the settlers. We find this in John Winthrop's *Arbella* sermon, the same address from which

Reagan takes his "city on a hill" line. Even while looking forward to their glorious success, the new settlers felt the burden of possible failure. Worried that the Puritans' expectations could make them greedy and overly concerned with earthly rewards to the exclusion of their Christian duty of charity and humility, Winthrop warned the emmigrants what could happen:

> The eyes of all people are upon us, so that if we shall deal falsely with our God in this work we have undertaken, and so cause him to withdraw his present help from us, we shall be made a story and a by-word through the world. We shall open the mouths of enemies to speak evil of the ways of God, and all professors for God's sake. We shall shame the faces of many of God's worthy servants, and cause their prayers to be turned into curses upon us until we be consumed out of the good land whither we are a going.

History would record with astonishment—to use the words that Reagan applied to the demise of democracy in "A Time for Choosing"—the shameful failure of the Puritan nation.

The Puritans soon found themselves at something of a loss when Christ did not arrive to rule them. Increasing prosperity and political freedom transformed the holy city upon a hill into an economic and civil paradise. "Puritanism," wrote Alexis de Tocqueville, became "almost as much a political theory as a religious doctrine." In the three and a half centuries since Winthrop and his people landed, the original theology of the Massachusetts Bay Colony has given way to a wide range of American civil religions.

Two general characteristics distinguish the jeremiad as it has been used in America, whether in a strictly religious sense or in one of its many political expressions. First, this country has a definite purpose for existing—some set of communal values, ideals, and goals that we group together and might call the American Dream; second, we live in continual risk of straying from the true path that God—or a political Founding Father—set for us.

But there is more to the American jeremiad than gloom and despair. As Sacvan Bercovitch explains in *The American Jeremiad,* the real message of this kind of communication is redemptive. Although in Old Testament Israel and in Europe the jeremiad did have a decidedly grim character, Bercovitch sees its American expression as looking finally beyond desolation to a paradise on earth:

> In explicit opposition to the traditional mode, it inverts the doctrine of vengeance into a promise of ultimate success, affirming to the world, and despite the world, the inviolability of the colonial cause. . . .
>
> In Europe, let me emphasize, the jeremiad pertained exclusively to mundane, social matters, to the city of man rather than the city of God. It required not conversion but moral obedience and civic virtue. At best, it held out the prospect of temporal, worldly success. At worst, it threatened not hellfire, but secular calamity (disease, destruction, death). The Puritans' concept of errand entailed a fusion of secular and sacred history. The purpose of their jeremiads was to direct an imperiled people of God toward the fulfillment of their destiny, to guide them individually toward salvation, and collectively toward the American city of God.[3]

Reagan does something fascinating with the jeremiad form; he combines the older emphasis on the city of man with his politicized Christianity. The President requires both earthly obedience and spiritual conversion. It is not enough for voters to cast their ballots according to Reagan's advice; they also must accept Reagan's sublime gospel of America's future destiny. And despite his reminders of the dreadful possibilities of failure, Reagan never fails to see a glorious tomorrow. Visions of despair aside, Ronald Reagan's rhetoric of the American Dream apotheosizes the people and the future of this land.

Reagan applies the tropes and strategies of his ultimate optimism to nearly every issue which he addresses, translating Christian regeneration into patriotism and civic duty. Speaking to the graduating class of the United States Military Academy at West point in 1981, the President described American history under the liberals as a dark night of the country's soul: "We've been through a period in which . . . there was an erosion of respect for the honorable profession that you have chosen." But a new day was dawning:

> Well, I'm happy to tell you that the people of America have re-covered from what can only be called a temporary aberration. There is a spiritual revival going on in this country, a hunger on the part of the people to once again be proud of America—all that it is and all that it can be. . . .
> Let friend and foe alike be made aware of the spirit that is sweeping across our land. . . . Very much a part of this new spirit is patriotism, and with that goes a heartfelt appreciation for the sacrifices of those in uniform.

The image of a national rebirth also pervades the President's addresses on the economy. Helping to celebrate the birthday of Alf Landon (against whom Reagan voted in the presidential election of 1936), he repeated his common statement about America being a promised land, only with an important variation: "I've always believed that this blessed land was set apart in a special way." he said. But this time he did not say that the first settlers came to the New World seeking "not for gold, but mainly in search of God." Instead the President described their goal as "something new in all the history of mankind—a land where man is not beholden to government; government is beholden to man." The prophecy of the New Jerusalem of Christianity be-came a quasi-religious endorsement of conservative politics.

Then Reagan used preacherly language to support his eco-nomic programs:

> You may have read the passage in the Psalms which says: "Weeping may endure for a night, but joy cometh in the morning." The Ameri-can people have endured a long and terrible night, lasting more than a decade and filled with one economic disappointment after another. And today, that long night is ending. We will see a new dawn of hope and opportunities for all our people.

The President went on in his next sentence to praise the tax reforms and spending reduction plans of his administration. The quotation comes from Psalm 30, in which King David of Israel thanks the Lord for keeping him strong and prosperous and rejoices that the anger of God passes quickly. There is a subliminal connection for those familiar with the Psalms—as many of Reagan's conservative supporters are—between liberal economic policies and the wrath of God visited upon his errant people.

The President also uses religious language to speak of private sector volunteerism. At the Landon celebration he hoped to see Americans "renewing our spirit of friendship, community service, and caring for the needy—a spirit that flows like a deep and mighty river through the history of our nation." The President may have had in mind the biblical keynote of the National Association of Evangelicals, which he quoted in his Orlando address, when he called for amendments on abortion and school prayer the previous March: "Yes, let justice roll on like a river, righteousness like a never-failing stream." In Dixon for his seventy-third birthday, Reagan saw community volunteerism as the inspiring answer to the country's woes. "Our faith was our strength," he said of Dixonites who suffered poverty during the Depression; "We knew . . . we would overcome adversity and that after the storm, the stars would come."

The sense of crusading comes through very pronouncedly in Reagan's speeches to cadres of conservative political workers. He frequently sounds as if he were the head of an embattled religious order, a church militant of the American government under long siege. "The conservative movement in twentieth century America held fast through hard and difficult years to its vision of truth," he said to the 1981 Conservative Political Action Conference. He described the men and women who had dedicated their lives to the resurgence of Goldwater conservatism as political priests, monks, and nuns: "[T]here are many in this room whose talents might have entitled them to a life of affluence," he said, "but who chose another career out of a higher sense of duty to country." After repeating the story of Whittaker Chambers, the

President characterized the work of conservatism as an evangelical mission:

> This is the real task before us: to reassert our commitment as a nation to a law higher than our own, to renew our spiritual strength. Only by building a wall of such spiritual resolve can we, as a free people, hope to protect our own heritage and make it someday that birthright of all men. . . .
>
> While we celebrate our recent political victory we must understand there's much work before us: . . . to make our own spiritual affirmation in the face of those who would deny man has a place before God.

And, of course, Reagan speaks of international politics in prophetic tones even when not addressing overtly religious audiences. One striking example of this practice is his address to the Spirit of America Rally, which he delivered three days before announcing his intention to seek a second term in the White House. The President ran through the usual elements of his platform: free market policies, reduced government, tax reductions, an amendment to balance the budget, school prayer, and community service, and then gave credit for America's revival to the inspired businessmen and women who follow his gospel in the marketplace:

> It's people like you who show us the heart of America is good, the spirit of America is strong, and the future of America is great. You give meaning to words like entrepreneur, self-reliance, personal initiative and, yes, optimism and confidence. And you will lead America to take freedom's next step. . . .
>
> We can make America stronger not just economically and militarily, but also morally and spiritually. We can make our beloved country the source of all the dreams and opportunities she was placed on this good Earth to provide. We need only to believe in each other and in the God who has so blessed our land.

We need only believe, said the President, in the gospel of the Reagan Crusade.

Running for reelection on the strength of his record and, more importantly, on the assertion that Americans had to renew the political and spiritual committment that they made in 1980, Reagan reminded us again and again of how close we had come to apostasy. Looking back to the state of the nation before his advent, Reagan said in his 1984 nomination acceptance address, "Americans were losing the confidence and optimism about the future that has made us unique in the world." With the Reagan regeneration, though, Americans renewed their compact with God by endorsing their president's political agenda:

The Poet called Miss Liberty's torch the "lamp beside the golden door." Well, that was the entrance to America, and it still is. And now you really know why we are here tonight.

The glistening hope of that lamp is still ours. Every promise, every opportunity is still golden in this land. And through that golden door our children can walk into tomorrow with the knowledge that no one can be denied the promise that is America.

Her heart is full; her door is still golden, her future bright. She has arms big enough to comfort and strong enough to support. For the strength in her arms is the strength of her people. She will carry on in the eighties unafraid, unashamed, and unsurpassed.

In this springtime of hope, some lights seem eternal; America's is.

Thank you, God bless you, and God bless America.

In 1964, facing Goldwater's defeat, Reagan concentrated on the dark side of the jeremiad. Twenty years later, with the odds heavily in his favor, the President turned to the optimistic vein identified by Bercovitch. Whether or not he is a born-again Christian of whatever stripe—and regardless, perhaps of our own religious opinions—Reagan's transformation of our earthly history into part of a divine destiny is an enormously successful rhetorical strategy. Heartfelt expression of a personal faith, or cynical manipulation of subliminal traditions, Reagan's use of the priestly mode works.

NOTES

1. Howell Rains, "Reagan Backs Evangelicals in Their Political Activities," *The New York Times*, August 23, 1980, p. A–8.
2. John Herbers, "Armageddon View Prompts a Debate," *The New York Times*, October 24, 1984, p. A–1.
3. Sacvan Bercovitch, *The American Jeremiad* (Madison: University of Wisconsin Press, 1975), pp. 7, 9.

6 / WHAT KIND OF PEOPLE ARE WE?

The election of 1984 was a struggle for the soul of America, fought rhetorically.

Accepting the nomination of his party in August, President Reagan described the struggle clearly: "The choices this year are not just between two different personalities or between two political parties," declared the President, "They're between two different visions of the future." In his speech to the Democrats, former Vice President Mondale spoke in a similar vein. "Over the next hundred days," he said, "in every word we say, in every life we touch, we will be fighting for America's future."

We can look at the election as a contest based on two versions of American history, similar yet distinct narratives offered for the acceptance of the electorate. Put simply, Reagan and Mondale had to convince the voters that their specific vision of America's past and future was the only true one, the sole gospel of the American Dream. Reagan cast Mondale as an apostate, and the challenger did the same to the President.

The debate also consisted of arguments over facts: Reagan and Mondale routinely pronounced each other abysmally ignorant and uninformed. Much more important, though, was each man's attempt to portray the other as out of touch with the more fundamental visionary truth of America's spiritual significance and character.

Ronald Reagan fired the first rhetorical volley of the 1984 campaign four days before he formally announced his intention to seek reelection. His State of the Union Address of January 25, ostensibly a report on the nation's material welfare, was a discourse on the character of America's history. At the very outset of his campaign, Reagan placed the election in the context of a vision of destiny and obligation. He opened by noting "that America is much improved, and there's good reason to believe that improvement will continue through the days to come." "There is renewed energy and optimism throughout the land," said Reagan, again suggesting that his government had restored us to previous greatness; "America is back, standing tall, looking to the eighties with courage, confidence, and hope."

Obviously, Reagan's speech was not simply a report on the state of the union in 1984 relative to that of 1983. As part of his race against Jimmy Carter's former Vice President, Reagan needed to concentrate on developments since his first election in 1980. He made this explicit:

As we came to the decade of the eighties, we faced the worst crisis of our postwar history. In the seventies were years of rising problems and falling confidence. There was a feeling government had grown beyond the consent of the governed. Families felt helpless in the face of mounting inflation and the indignity of taxes that reduced reward for hard work, thrift, and risk-taking. All this was overlaid by an ever-growing web of rules and regulations.

On the international scene, we had an uncomfortable feeling that we'd lost the respect of friend and foe. Some questioned whether we had the will to defend peace and freedom.

In the 1970s, especially, according to Reagan, between 1976 and 1980, American history went awry; along with the almost physical obstacles and hindrances of federal paperwork and bureaucracy, the country suffered deeply from a crisis of faith. And faith, as we know, is the first requirement of success in Reagan's gospel. By refusing the look beyond the petty concerns and worries, by not embracing the transcendent vision of America's destiny, the liberal Carter and Mondale had plunged the country into a crisis. "But America is too great for small dreams," said President Reagan in a line recalling his celebration of our imaginative capacity in his 1981 inaugural:

There was a hunger in the land for a spiritual revival; if you will, a crusade for renewal. The American people said: Let us look to the future with confidence, both at home and abroad. Let us give freedom a chance.

The bulk of Reagan's state of the union address consisted of such pep-rally-like exhortations. "The cynics were wrong," he said; "America never was a sick society." After running through a list of achievements and goals and making predictable statements about his desires for peace, prosperity, and so forth, the President concluded his preannouncement but de facto campaign oration by calling on his countrymen to ignore those of little faith in the Democratic leadership. The language is familiar:

How can we not believe in the greatness of America? How can we not do what is right and needed to preserve this last best hope of man on Earth? After all our struggles to restore America, to revive confidence in our country, hope for the future, after all our hard-won victories earned through the patience and courage of every citizen, we cannot, must not, and will not turn back. We will finish our job.

Notice how Reagan intertwined talk of tangible achievements (the restoration of America and hard-won victories) with concern for our emotional and spiritual condition. The state of the American people, as described by President Reagan in this address, was prosperous, healthy, and—above all—devoutly faithful to our national mission. Not only had we solved particular mundane problems; we had under this President regenerated our belief in ourselves and renewed our quasi-divine covenant. Reagan's first speech of the 1984 campaign was a decidely cheerful expression. We have found the true way once again and are back on the path of righteousness.

Reagan echoed the themes of his achievement in his official announcement, bringing his audience into his narrative of recent years. "Together we've faced many difficult problems," the President told us, "and I've come to feel a special bond of kinship with each of you." As he did in the State of the Union speech—and as he would continue to do throughout the campaign—Reagan recalled the dismal conditions he found on entering the White House in 1981, then rhapsodized about improvements. "Well, things have changed," he said; "As I said Wednesday night, America is back and standing tall. We've begun to restore great American values—the dignity of work, the warmth of family, the strength of neighborhood, and the nourishment of human freedom." He proclaimed the voters "the real heroes of American democracy," calling us "magnificent as we pulled the Nation through the long night of our national calamity." Reagan's Americans in 1984 were a supremely confident people.

Challenging an enormously popular President during a time of evident peace and prosperity, the Democrats worked hard in 1984 to convince the electorate that only they understood the genuine nature of Americans and that their portrayal of the voters as characters in a liberal narrative captured reality. Mario Cuomo sounded this theme explicitly in his keynote address at the Democratic National Convention in July. "This election will measure the record of the past four years," he declared. "But more than that, it will answer the question of what kind of people we want to be."[1] Cuomo's very words proved essential to the Democrats' rhetorical strategy. Geraldine Ferraro's basic stump speech echoed Cuomo's address: "This election will also be a referendum on what kind of people we are," she told audiences across the nation. And Walter Mondale raised the question in nearly every speech. As he told an audience in Peoria, Illinois on September 12, "The question in this campaign we must ask is, What kind of people are we as Americans?"

Basing much of their attack on scenes of poverty, prejudice, and fear, the Democrats described Americans as compassionate witnesses and participants not in a glorious success, but in a potentially tragic scenario. "We're fair," was how Mondale characterized us in Peoria, Illinois, on September 12,

We're decent. We're kind. And we're caring. We insist that, as we care for ourselves, there are some in America who need our help. . . . There's a limit to what Americans will permit to happen in this good country of ours. We are a nation that cares.

The essence of the Democratic appeal seemed to be to convince the voters that things were bad and people badly off. Americans, they said, were just not the kind of people who could allow someone as heartless as Ronald Reagan to stay in the White House. Of course, President Reagan had his own answer to the question of national identity posed by the Democrats. The portrait that he offered to Americans pleased them enough to earn him a massive victory at the polls. While Mondale and Ferraro told us that we were a concerned and cautious nation, the President gave a gloriously reassuring description of his countrymen. Reagan knew both sides of the argument. Out of power he spoke grimly; running for reelction, he was nothing but optimistic.

Even as Mondale, Ferraro, and their Democratic supporters were trying to make their story heard, President Reagan was telling the voters something quite different. In June of 1984, Assistant White House Chief of Staff Richard Darman wrote a memorandum on the upcoming campaign in which he captured the essence of Reagan's rhetorical strategy. "Paint Mondale as . . . soft in his defense of freedom, patriotic values, American interests," advised Darman; *"Paint RR as the personification of all that is right with or heroized by America.* Leave Mondale in a position where an attack on Reagan is tantamount to an attack on America's idealized image of itself—*where a vote against Reagan is in some subliminal sense, a vote against mythic 'AMERICA'."*[2] Darman's advice fit perfectly with the Reagan tradition of turning politics into myth and religion. Reagan and his staff did exactly what Darman urged, and they did it well. On his very first campaign trip after the Democratic convention, Reagan addressed a rally in Atlanta, accusing the liberals of distorting one of the most famous lines of perhaps their most mythic spokesman. In fact, Reagan was the one distorting the language of Franklin Roosevelt: "The future, according to [the Democrats], is dark and getting darker, and Americans are very unhappy. According to the other party, there's nothing to hope for but despair, and we have nothing in store but fear itself." Under the Carter-Mondale administration, Reagan asserted, "American prestige seemed like a memory. Our standing in the world had fallen. Our government was talking about a malaise. You remember that talk, and you were the ones that were supposed to be having the malaise."

The plain truth is there's a mood in this country, a general feeling that, indeed, America is a decent and a just place, and it deserves our love and fidelity.

There's a mood, a general feeling that patriotism isn't something to be embarassed about, but something to be proud of. There's a mood in the country, a general feeling that once again there's a lot to be hopeful about. Our optimism has once again been turned loose. And all of us recognize that these people who keep talking about the age of limits, are really talking about their own limitations, not America's.

In invoking the revival of pride and optimism that he saw in America, Reagan was referring to what has been called "the New Patriotism." The elements (and even the reality) of this purported wave of nationalism have yet to be analyzed as completely as they might. In essence, it consisted of such diverse phenomena as a rise in the sales figures for American flags, enthusiasm for the American Olympic athletes, and a general resurrection of nationalist spirit that presumably had been absent since the antiwar demonstrations of the Vietnam era or since the Carter years, depending on one's interpretation. Quite possibly, the New Patriotism may have been what Daniel Boorstin called a "pseudoevent," as much a product of media hyperbole as of any genuine popular emotion. Whatever its nature, entrepreneurs lost no time in taking advantage of the phenomenon. The year 1984 saw an abundance of "patriotic" products—T-shirts, bumper stickers, workout clothes, and the like—bearing the "U.S.A." logo. Patriotic motifs appeared frequently in advertising, and a television network debuted a new series about the military during the Vietnam War, "Call to Glory." No stranger to such methods, The Great Communicator also noted and took advantage of the apparent frenzy:

Journalists have described and analyzed this outpouring of unity and positive feeling. They also noted that this year's Fourth of July celebrations were extraordinarily joyous occasions. There is a new patriotism spreading across our country. It's an affection for our way of life, expressed by people who represent the width and breadth of our culturally diverse society. And the new patriotism is not a negative force that excludes, but a positive force, an attitude toward those things that are fundamental to America, that draws together our freedom, our decency, our sense of fair play as a people.

For reasons that hardly need explaining, a wave of revived patriotism could work wonders for an incumbent president.

To create and communicate his vision of Americans as a

powerful and buoyant people, Reagan used the full range of rhetorical devices and motifs that he had developed over his long career as a politician. His reelection oratory is overwhelmingly rich in symbolic language evocative of the New Patriotism. One important element of Reagan's description of Americans as a people of reborn nationalism consisted quite naturally of praise for our renewed military profile. His final campaign appeal, a radio broadcast of November 5, contained all the standard tropes of patriotic pride. Reagan credited the American people for their greatness. "The greatness of America doesn't begin in Washington"; he said, "it begins with each of you—in the mighty spirit of a free people under God, in the bedrock values you live by each day in your families, neighborhoods and workplaces." There followed a long program of proud moments and stirring words, culminating in his contention that Americans had seen "a change from only those few years ago when patriotism seemed out of style." Then Mr. Reagan presented three military related scenes:

I'm not sure anyone really knows when this new patriotism began or how it grew so quickly. Was its seed first planted that day our P.O.W.'s who had braved a horrendous captivity in North Vietnam, came home and said, "God bless America?" . . .

We've known great joy—as when we welcomed back our soldiers and those students from Grenada—but also enduring grief from the loss of brave men—on the Grenada rescue mission and on our peacekeeping mission in Beirut. Each gave his life for a noble cause. Each must be remembered and honored—forever.

I treasure a memory of a visit to Normandy, where I met the boys of Pointe du Hoc. And later at Omaha Beach, I read from the letter of a loving daughter who had promised her father, a Normandy veteran, that someday she would go back there for him. She would see the beaches and visit the monuments and place flowers at the graves of his fallen comrades. "I'll never forget," she wrote. And, "Dad, I'll always be proud.'"

President Reagan made certain that the American people knew that they were a tough nation and that he would stand up for their rights and interests. "Uncle Sam is a friendly old man," he warned, "but he has a spine of steel." Invoking memories of the hostages held by Iran, Reagan predicted Mondale would make us "a nation that begs on its knees for kindness from tyrants." Mondale, according to Reagan, saw a world in which "America is the victim, flinching under the blows of history." But thanks to the New Patriotism, "Gone are the days when we meekly tolerated obvious threats to our peace and security." This revitalized ability and willingness to develop and to flex our military muscles came directly, according to Reagan, from our national character. This passage, notable for its curious and circular pseudo-logic, comes from the standard peroration that Reagan used in the last days of the campaign:

Ours is the home of the free because it is the home of the brave. Our future will always be great because our nation will always be strong. Our nation will be strong because we're free. And our people will be free because we're united—one people under God, with liberty and justice for all.

Examining the components of the statement above, we find that freedom depends on courage, strength, and the national character as a happy, inspired, and united people. Success requires that Americans believe in Reagan's characterization of them and that they be willing to play the parts he writes for them. Those who see things otherwise threaten our "unity" and undermine our might. "I think of your patriotism," President Reagan told veterans, "and I just have to wonder: How can anyone [presumably Mondale] not believe that the heart of America is good, that the spirit of America is strong, and that the future of America is great?"

Even though he ran on a platform of strong military ability and readiness, declaring America "a giant on the scene," President

Reagan had to beware of seeming too bellicose. Many Americans had a real fear of excessive militarism in the summer of 1984, and the events of those days, including the bombings in Beirut, the absence of negotiations with the Soviets, increased presence in Central America highlighted by revelations of a C. I. A. instruction manual on assassination, and the President's own unfortunate joke about bombing the Russians in five minutes. They increased the chances that Reagan could sound too strong. He needed a way to talk about America's strength and confidence as manifested in our competitive insistence on victory, without going on at length about the military. Reagan found that a good means to do this was to humanize the members of the armed services as symbolic characters, even while bragging about how much more professional they had become. He turned helmeted soldiers and pilots into stereotypes of the country—clean-cut, All Americans. On several occasions he climaxed his praise for the military by quoting General George Marshall, the epitome of a beneficent military, who when asked what secret weapon would bring him victory, replied, "The best damn kids in the world."

An even more effective technique than that of emphasizing a strong military ability was to present an alternative vision of American youth as athletes. Beyond any others, sports imagery pervades Reagan's campaign oratory, and his strong and competitive young athletes are a transparently if unconsciously coded presentation of the aggressive and defiant traits of militarism of which he had to be wary. One of the earliest and most striking motifs in Reagan's campaign rhetoric was that of the Los Angeles Olympic Games. The same magazines, newspapers, and all-important television screens that proclaimed the patriotic revival also gave us in the summer of 1984 innumerable images of determined young men and women dressed in red, white, and blue running shorts and leotards and bedecked with gold, silver, and occasionally bronze medals. Reagan and his campaign advisors, with their well-developed skill for associating the President with symbolic moments and situations—the same instinct that makes for good "photo opportunities," some might say—moved swiftly to transform the international competition into a celebration of their America and of the Reagan administration. The President spent the election surrounded with images of triumph.

Reagan gave three speeches that specifically concerned the Olympics, each intertwining praise for the athletes with his joyful portrait of the American people: a radio address to the nation on the opening day (July 28, only a week after the Democrats adjourned in San Francisco), a speech to U.S. Athletes on the same day, and a congratulatory address at a victory breakfast on August 12. In marked contrast to Mondale's sombre message, Reagan's speeches resounded with cheer and pride. "There are many serious things that will occupy our attention in the coming weeks and in the fall," he told the nation on opening day—not too subtly placing the games in the context of the election even as he ostensibly set them apart. "But today I find my thoughts turning away from politics to something equally important but happy, too." Describing the journey of the Olympic torch across the United States, President Reagan pictured America as anything but the country of suffering, unfairness, and despair:

> I'm thinking of what journey it knew, and what a country it traveled through. . . .
> It was carried by former Olympians and handicapped kids, by elderly women and young athletes bright with the speed of youth.
> They held the torch high and passed the flame on to one another. They took it up hills and through lonely towns in the darkness, along gray highways at twilight and through bright towns at noon.

Young and old, handicapped and hale, the torch bearers embodied America, working together in a common splendid effort. Persistent and stalwart enough to climb heights and cross dark towns, the runners stood quite obviously for a people determined to win. "Everywhere the torch went," he said, "people came out of their homes and poured into the streets to cheer and wave the flag and urge the runners on."

The athletes also represented the campaigning President. "Today it begins," he said, conjuring up moments of anticipation as athletes poised themselves on starting lines awaiting the starting gun. "Our young people are running for their country," Reagan said, "running for greatness, for achievement, for that moving thing in man that makes him push on to the impossible." Although the athletes would do more than *run* in Los Angeles—they would swim, jump, dive, ride, vault, and more—Reagan had a perfect reason to stress *running*: his own *running* for reelection. Apart from his quick promise at the outset of the address not to speak of the election, Reagan said nothing about his own race; but the campaign pervaded his speech. The subtext was clear: America was eager to cheer on Ronald Reagan and his Republican team as they won their own gold medals. In his opening-day address to the American athletes themselves, President Reagan invoked his familiar alter ego, the Gipper. "Set your sights high," he told the competitors, "and then go for it. For yourselves, for your family, for your country—and will you forgive me if I just be a little presumptious—'do it for the Gipper.'"

The impressively high number of victories won by U.S. athletes—victories made slightly less real by the absence of athletes from the Soviets and their allies—increased the metaphoric value of the Olympics to Reagan's campaign. By taking symbolic credit for the triumphs, President Reagan could turn each American gold medal into votes for his reelection. Reflecting at the postgame breakfast celebration on how he believed the world perceived Americans by way of internationally televised broadcasts of the games, the President told us what kind of people we are:

I couldn't help but think that if the people of the world judged Americans by what they saw of you, then they think, "Americans? Well, they're generous and full of serious effort; they're full of high spirits;

they're motivated by all the best things. They're truly a nation of champions.

President Reagan spoke of the Olympics all through his campaign, rarely missing an opportunity to tell Americans that they were "a nation of champions." His nomination-acceptance address in Dallas on August 23, a pastiche of familiar Reaganesque motifs and lines, climaxed in a moving peroration built around the games. Telling the convention (and the nation, who watched on television) that under his leadership the American people "came together in a national crusade to make America great again, and to make a new beginning," he proclaimed the campaign months "a springtime of hope" that began with the Olympics. "Holding the Olympic games here in the United States," announced the President, "began defining the promise of this season."

With the audience cheering, "U.S.A.! U.S.A.! U.S.A.!" President Reagan found in his Olympic imagery one of his favorite rhetorical motifs, the flame of freedom and hope that burns in the hearths of Iowa and that throws light on Berlin. Expanding on the picture he had described in Atlanta of the Olympic torch crossing the United States, Reagan tied the entire nation together in one grand metaphoric quest for victory in Los Angeles:

> In Richardson, Texas, it was carried by a 14-year old boy in a special wheelchair. In West Virginia the runner came across a line of deaf children and let each one pass the torch for a few feet, and at the end these youngsters' hands talked excitedly in their sign language. Crowds spontaneously began singing, "America the Beautiful" or "The Battle Hymn of the Republic."
>
> Then in San Francisco a Vietnamese immigrant, his little son held on his shoulders, dodged photographers and policemen to cheer a 19-year-old black man pushing an 88-year-old white woman in a wheelchair as she carried the torch.

The convention roaring, television cameras trained on tearful, beaming faces, President Reagan declared, "My friends, that's America."

Allusions to the Olympics were continued right up to the election. Reagan praised students at Jefferson Junior High as "our Olympians of the classroom," and told an audience in Detroit that when he arrived in Washington the government "stopped singing out 'S.O.S.' and started saying, 'U.S.A.'" "We were never meant to be a second best nation," the President told gatherings across the country; "And so, like our Olympic athletes, we're going to go for the gold."

The Olympic motif fits Ronald Reagan's long fondness for sports both on the field and in his rhetoric. Hardly a speaking engagement took place during Reagan's campaign without one sporting metaphor or another. Arriving in Dallas for his nomination, he complimented Texans in general and the Dallas Cowboys in particular for their winning ways. "You don't just score victories," he said, "you romp 'em." He called the Cowboys "America's team," then predicted that by the end of the week, the Republicans would become "America's party." On the morning after the first debate with Walter Mondale, Reagan said that it had been "a litte sparring in the political arena . . . for the soul of this country and the will of its people." In the closing days of the campaign, working to help Republicans get elected to the Senate and House, Reagan became George Gipp again, imploring voters to "help spread the word, get out the vote, and win 'em for the Gipper." He characterized himself and Mondale as two men contending for the head-coach position of the American team:

Well, making our economy bear the burden of [Mondale's promised] tax hike would be like having a coach tell an Olympic swimmer to do the laps with a ball and chain. Come November, the American people are going to get to vote on their coaches. And come November, the American people are going to tell Coach Tax Hike to go find another team someplace else.

What does all this sports talk mean in terms of Reagan's idea of what kind of people we are? Every characteristic of the athletes in his speeches transfers directly to his protrayal of Americans in 1984. We were, he told us, optimistic, determined, fit, brave, and destined for victory—so long as we did not fall for the Democrats' notion that we were otherwise. Above all, Reagan depicted America as a nation of *winners*. Of course, only one person can win a race; there must be losers as well. Who would lose in Reagan's meta-Olympic games? Anyone who failed to join his team, the Democrats, persons who foolishly refused to believe in his visions, and, naturally, our enemies abroad. The President revealed just how much his talk about sports, Olympic and otherwise, was a metaphor for his vision of America as an international giant. This passage comes from an address in Sedalia, Missouri:

> We're strong because we believe in a bedrock principle: We are a government of, by, and for the people, not the other way around. And we're strong because we know that true greatness begins with the deepest treasures of the human spirit, with faith and courage, with loyalty and love, with a quiet, unselfish devotion to our families, our neighbors, and our nation.
>
> I couldn't help but think of these things as I watched our Olympic athletes. Didn't you get the feeling that the Soviets must have been relieved when the closing ceremonies for the Olympics were over? But one thing they'll never see is closing ceremonies for America.

This transformation of the Olympics from an athletic event into a surrogate for international competition between America and the Evil Empire of the Soviets certainly corresponds to the feeling many people have about such sporting events. We need only recall how we responded to the victory of the United States hockey team over their Soviet opponents at the 1980 Lake Placid Olympics—a win often referred to by Reagan as proof of our superior spirit—to see this clearly.

While Reagan told us from the earliest days of his campaign that we were the kind of people who rejoiced in our strength and success, the Democrats offered a far less strident portrait. As we have noted, they began by telling us about our concern and compassion. Vowing that his party had to make its case "not so much with speeches that bring people to their feet as with speeches that bring people to their senses," Mario Cuomo sounded this basic liberal theme in his keynote address at the convention. He struck right for the heart of Reagan's myth of America by turning one of the President's favorite symbols upside down. According to Cuomo, Reagan had recently admitted that some Americans remained wretched even in the apparently joyous summer of 1984; but, again according to Cuomo, the President had said he that didn't understand why, and had claimed, "Why, this country is a shining city on a hill." Governor Cuomo insisted that America was more a "Tale of Two Cities."

The Governor denounced Reagan's New Jerusalem of peace and wealth as a cruel fiction. Commenting on some of the rhetorical terms used to describe Reagan's shimmering vistas, Cuomo described miserable neighborhoods in the shining city. "There are people who sleep in the city's streets, where the glitter doesn't show," he said; "There is despair, Mr. President, in faces you never see, in places you never visit in your shining city." Offering scenes of poverty, ruin, and fear in grim contrast to Reagan's speeches, Cuomo substituted allusions to Dickensian squalor for Reagan's joyful vignettes. Reagan's American Dreamers made up a tiny rich minority of Americans, he said, who could not see the real people and state of the nation from their lofty penthouses. Reagan offered nothing but "the same shining city for those relative few who are lucky enough to live in its good neighborhoods. But for the people who are excluded—locked out—all they can do is stare from a distance at that city's glimmering towers."

The Democratic keynote proposed that those Americans who

did not actually live in misery remained keenly aware of and distressed about the conditions of their deprived fellows. Cuomo offered a Democratic alternative to Reagan's scenes of athletes racing across the country and around the Olympic track to limitless victories. It was itself based on an old American story motif:

The Republicans believe that wagon train will not make it to the frontier unless some of our old, some of our young and some of our weak are left behind by the side of the trail.

The strong will inherit the land!

We Democrats believe that we can make it all the way with the whole family intact.

We have. More than once.

Ever since Franklin Roosevelt lifted himself from his wheelchair to lift this nation from its knees. Wagon train after wagon train. To new frontiers of education, housing, peace. The whole family aboard. Constantly reaching out to extend and enlarge that family. Lifting them up into the wagon on the way. Blacks and Hispanics, people of every ethnic background, and Native Americans—all those struggling to build their families claim some small share of America.

Repeating the themes of Roosevelt's New Deal, Kennedy's New Frontier, and Johnson's Great Society, the Democratic leaders in 1984 emphasized again and again their concept of Americans as a people willing to help others less fortunate than themselves even if that meant moving more slowly into the future than they might otherwise. Having told voters that they truly cared about hardships and suffering, Cuomo and the Democrats went on to portray grim and touching scenes of poverty, unfairness, and fear in this country and abroad. "We have come far enough for now," their message seemed to be, "it is time to pause, to help stragglers into the wagon before moving on." Not all was right with America, Cuomo contended, and both the people and the Democratic party realized this and saw it as the overwhelming fact about America in 1984.

During the campaign months of 1984, the press and various other commentators devoted a good deal of attention to Walter Mondale's search for a "message"—a marketable set of positions and slogans that could be used to comprise a successful rhetoric. His campaign suffered from many false starts and pitfalls, including the failure to impose Bert Lance on the Democratic National Committee (as well, perhaps, as the very effort), the distressful events surrounding Congresswoman Ferraro's finances, and seemingly endless problems in organization. Along with these troubles, Mondale and his advisors appeared to flail about without direction. The debate centered around whether Mondale should stick to the basic liberal platform outlined by Cuomo, or "Reaganize" his rhetoric and come on tougher. It was a confused campaign at times, but on the whole Mondale stayed true to his compassionate vision of Americans, although expressing it in sterner terms than he might have had he not been competing with Reagan's message of optimism and might.

Mondale injected a note of pugnacity into the campaign with the very first sentence of his own address to the convention. "My fellow Americans," he said, "I accept your nomination—and I welcome the fight that comes with it." Admitting that Reagan "beat the pants" off Carter and Mondale in 1980, he promised "a new realism: ready for the future, and recapturing the best in our tradition." Mondale gave special prominence to defense and to a reduction of federal generosity:

We know that America must have a strong defense, and a sober view of the Soviets.

We know that government must be as well-managed as it is well-meaning.

We know that a healthy, growing private economy is the key to our future.

We know that Harry Truman spoke the truth: A President . . . has to able to say "yes" and "no" and more often "no."

Look at our platform. There are no defense cuts that weaken our security; no business taxes that weaken our economy; no laundry lists that raid our treasury.

Eager to counter suspicions that he would sell out America's military in order to buy off special-interest groups, Mondale reached out with his words not just to a people of concern and mercy, but also to Reagan's Americans. Mondale continued in this vein, promising that his deficit reduction tax plan would "get our competitive edge back," and "make America No. 1 again." He used strikingly belligerent words, telling countries that restricted our imports, "We will not be pushed around any more. We will have a President who stands up for American workers and American businesses and American farmers."

This appeal to a competitive American people was continued throughout Mondale's campaign, manifested not least in the banners proclaiming him "Fightin' Fritz." At times Mondale seemed to be speaking not to those American people described by Cuomo, but to the countrymen of Ronald Reagan. Praise of reduced government, religious values, a strengthened defense, pride in the military, and crime enforcement became prominent in Mondale's speeches. He even took to citing the Olympic athletes as symbols of the country's new competitiveness.

Geraldine Ferraro also followed this strategy to a large extent. In her standard text, she spoke at great length about social issues, but reminded audiences that as a prosecutor in New York City she "put [her] share of criminals behind bars." And in her debate with Vice President George Bush, she appeared even more dedicated to military power than her opponent did. Asked if her gender would prevent her from dealing forcefully with the Soviet Union, she answered with a stern demeanor:

Quite frankly I'm prepared to do whatever is necessary in order to secure this country and make sure that security is maintained.

Secondly, if the Soviet Union were to ever believe that they could challenge the United States with any sort of nuclear forces or otherwise, if I were in a position of leadership in this country, they would be assured that they would be met with swift, concise and certain retaliation.

Did the Democrats abandon their own traditionally liberal view of Americans for the sake of the New Patriotism rhetoric thinly disguised as "new realism?" No. They had just added a new dimension to their centrist-liberal vision. The statement with which Walter Mondale closed his remarks in the foreign policy debate of October 21 illustrates this synthesis. Earlier in the evening Mondale had accused Reagan of weakness—notably in the Mideast, where he saw "the United States left in humiliation and our enemies . . . stronger." As the debate ended, Mondale spoke to Americans characterized by concern over social welfare and the nuclear arms race. "I want a nation of fairness," he said,

where no one is denied the fullness of life or discriminated against, and we feel compassionately with those in our midst who are in trouble.

And above all, I want a nation that's strong. Since we debated two weeks ago, the United States and the Soviet Union have built more than one hundred more warheads, enough to kill millions of Americans and millions of Soviets.

This doesn't strengthen us, this weakens the chances of civilization to survive.

Mondale defined "strength" in terms of fairness and compromise, adopting some of the words and motifs of Reagan's oratory, but keeping his own fundamental premises. In a major address at George Washington University on September 25, he commented on how people perceived his campaign. "I have been advised to ignore issues—to choose slogans over substance," he said,

My answer is no. There is a big difference distance between Pennsylvania Avenue and Madison Avenue. And there ought to be a big difference between a Presidential election and a pep rally.

I have been counseled to cut loose from my history—to desert the forgotten Americans I have always fought for. My answer is no. I would rather lose a race about decency than win one about self-interest. I would rather fight for the heart and soul of America than fight for the bonuses of the *Fortune* 500.

Mondale turned back to his original question about the nature of Americans. "When the true story of this election is written, I suspect it will not be about me, or Mr. Reagan—but about you." Mondale vowed, "This election is about our values. . . . That's the kind of people we are." In essence, Mondale told Americans that they had troubles and that they could see those problems and that they would act true to their compassionate hearts. He told them to "Pick a President who hurts when you hurt." Ronald Reagan declared everything splendid, then smiled in the confidence that the people would choose him as the embodiment of their national self-image, as a President who felt as good as they did.

NOTES

1. All quotations from Democratic candidates other than Walter Mondale come from transcripts printed in *The New York Times*; citations of Mondale are from transcripts provided to me by the Mondale-Ferraro campaign staff.
2. *Newsweek: Election Extra: AVALANCHE* Vol. CIV, No. 21 November/December 1984, p. 88.

7 / THE SEMBLANCE OF POLITICS

Reagan won and Mondale lost. In overwhelming numbers, Americans saw themselves not in the challenger's words, but in the incumbent President's gloriously prophetic visions. And so, what kind of people are we, we who have elected the Great Communicator to the White House twice? What does the rhetoric of 1984 and of Mr. Reagan's two and a half decades of political life tell us about ourselves? First, the symbols, stories, and heroes that Reagan uses to connect so deeply with us reveal our wish to be, as he has said, "a giant on the scene." The people of America in the first half of the 1980s gazed approvingly at his depiction of us as a pious, strong, aggressively competitive, winning society basking in the grace of a beneficent God. Reagan's speeches resemble the paintings of Norman Rockwell in their portrayal of simple, cleanly drawn, and unconfused men and women.

Second, the reaction to the rhetoric that Reagan uses reveals our great frustration in life. This stems from our very inability to comprehend the world and to act clearly in our lives. Acting as intellectual, moral, and psychological surrogates, our leaders allegorically act to resolve for us this frustration. The majority of Americans in 1980 and 1984 perceived Jimmy Carter as a terribly weak president, not in the least because he let us see how burdensome the complexities of his office could be. When Mondale and others attacked Reagan's command of facts, when they reminded us, for example, that the President had erroneously said that submarine-launched missiles could be recalled, we seemed not to care. Famous for his mistakes, Reagan has misspoken enough times to fill a book with foolish, spurious statements. Yet these many revelations showing that the President clearly does not have the kind of superhuman control that we usually demand of our chief executives has had little effect on his popularity. President Reagan seems to remain unconcerned about charges that he, like the rest of us, has an incomplete grasp on the world. He takes long vacations from the White House, leaves difficult matters requiring expertise to his aides, and goes home from the Oval Office after short days to his television set. He even, we learned during the campaign, occasionally falls asleep during Cabinet meetings.

Far from provoking a majority of Americans into rejecting a President who failed just as much as they did to understand the ultimate complex facts of our world, the nation applauded Mr. Reagan and returned him to office in November, 1984. Why? On one hand, the state of the economy seemed sound—although a series of ominous statistics rumbled beneath Reagan's rhetoric throughout the campaign. Yet, I think that an even more important explanation lies in the grand message that Reagan offered us.

We believed him because he told us to, and because we wanted to. Our response to Reagan's rhetoric suggests that we are not an especially thoughtful or analytic nation of political readers, but a people seeking eagerly for answers, rather than for questions.

Ronald Reagan has attributed the New Patriotism to a resto- ration of "traditional values" after what he considers the social collapse of the Vietnam years, the Watergate crisis, and other disillusioning experiences. Perhaps the most telling of these "values" is faith, not just in God in this case, but faith in a vision of a world that does make sense. The discoveries of the late 1960s and 1970s—that Lyndon Johnson planned to escalate the war even while denying his intentions, for example, and that Richard Nixon was "a crook" despite his protests—brought us face to face with disillusionment. Recalling Daniel Boorstin's advice that we should disillusion ourselves about heroes and history, we might see the New Patriotism not so much as a celebration of genuine accomplishments, but as an orgy of re-illusionment. The people of America sought and continue to seek, in other words, a Great Communicator to reassure and to comfort them in a priestly as well as in a political sense. Fleeing from cold facts to soothing rhetoric, we show our vanity and our insecurity. If we look at the rhetoric of 1984 in terms of the jeremiad as explained by Ber- covitch, we see that while Walter Mondale stressed our failings and warned of dire consequences, President Reagan focused in- stead on the splendid prospect of a New Jerusalem in the here and now. In a world that despite its many pleasures, has in its heart an ever-present vision of nuclear annihilation, we reach out of nightmare into the glorious dreams of a perfect America.

Not surprisingly, the question of rhetorical deception and be- lievability played an important part in the national debate of 1984. Cuomo opened his speech to the Democratic convention with an explicit rejection of Reagan's communicative devices. "Please allow me to skip the stories and the poetry and the temp- tation to deal in nice but vague rhetoric," he asked; "Let me instead use this valuable opportunity to deal with questions that should determine this election and that are vital to the American people." Let Reagan imagine whatever pastoral landscapes he could, argued Cuomo; Democrats would look hard at facts. He continued:

> In order to succeed, we must answer our opponent's polished and appealing rhetoric with a more telling reasonableness and rationality.
> We must win this case on its merits.
> We must get the American public to look past the glitter, beyond the showmanship—to reality, to the hard substance of things. And we will do that not so much with speeches that sound good as with speeches that are good and sound.
> Not so much with speeches that bring people to their feet as with speeches that bring people to their senses.

Mondale also castigated Reagan's rhetoric all through his campaign. Speaking in Lansing, Michigan, on September 14, he said, "Given a choice between hearing the truth and listening to hoakum, the American people always want it straight." And in the final days of his doomed race, Mondale said that Reagan's speeches and television commercials were "all picket fences and puppy dogs. No one's hurting. No one's alone. No one's hungry. No one's unemployed. No one gets old. Everybody's happy." As Michael Ford, Mondale's field coordinator observed: "[Reagan] is Winesburg Ohio. . . . We are Cleveland. . . . Winesburg, of course, never existed."[1] *Winesburg, Ohio* is, though, avidly read; Anderson's novel captures America's (perhaps illusory) sense of itself much more completely than many history books do.

Of course, Reagan in turn criticized the Democrats for their false rhetoric. On his first trip out of the White House after his opponents accused him, in their convention, of obfuscation, the President responded not only to the substantive points, but also joined the contest over language. The San Francisco convention produced some powerful oratory that was far from purely exposi-

119

tory after all: Cuomo and Jesse Jackson gave inspiring emotional addresses and even Modale's shorter and more prosaic acceptance speech had an effective straight-forwardness. Well aware of what good speeches could do, Reagan wasted no time in dismissing Democratic oratory. He began the counterattack at a rally in Atlanta on July 26th:

> You know those folks who are writing off the South out there in the fog in San Francisco, they were busy talking and filling the air with eloquent-sounding words; as a matter of fact, big clouds of words. But a lot of those words contained what Winston Churchill called "terminological inexactitude." That's a nice way of saying they said a few things that weren't true. . . .
>
> Well, it was great dramatic rhetoric, but the fog has cleared, and this is a good time to look at the record, to look at the facts.

For years Reagan has characterized liberals as people of much talk and no action, as "tiny men with shrill voices" whose chatter and whining just got in the way of the true fulfillment of America's destiny. Everything that Reagan said in his reelection campaign had roots in the anti-intellectual, stridently middle-class rhetoric of his earlier career. On the same day that he described Democratic oratory as so much fog, something bothersome but basically harmless, Mr. Reagan characterized the language of his opponents as something actually quite dangerous. Echoing his many statements linking liberals with totalitarianism, the President warned an audience in Elizabeth, New Jersey to be on their guard. "Well, this is 1984," he said,

> and we might remember George Orwell's warning about '84, that "if thought corrupts language, language can also corrupt thought." Others may try to fool the public. Our campaign will be one of clear thinking and honest talk with the American people.

This passage comes, in fact, not from 1984, but from Orwell's essay, "Politics and the English Language," in which he was not warning about 1984 but commenting on what he considered a general problem in the reliability of political communication. Orwell's essay rejected the kind of talismanic rhetoric which both Republicans and Democrats produced in 1984. He saw in trite and inexact language not simply bad or unpleasant style, but a reduction of important intellectual processes to a fairly automatic stimulus-response exchange. "Modern writing at its worst does not consist in picking out words for the sake of their meaning and inventing images in order to make the meaning clearer," explained Orwell; "It consists in gumming together long strips of words which have already been set in order by someone else, and making the results presentable by sheer humbug." Orwell went on to say that bad political language "is designed to make lies sound truthful and murder respectable, and to give an appearance of solidity to wind."[2] This complaint about the public language of the late 1940s applies disturbingly well to that of our own day as well. Nearly all of what we heard in the election of 1984, from liberal and conservative alike, deserves dismissal as "just so much rhetoric," as little more than established symbols clearly defined for both speaker and audience. Reading all of Reagan's presidential speeches and a good deal of his work from years before 1981, we discover a remarkable paucity of vocabulary. As we have noted, he relies on a small set of rhetorical devices: the same jokes, anecdotes, characters, and motifs turn up again and again in his oratory.

Socrates denounced the professional speechmakers and teachers of oratory in Athens as linguistic prostitutes whose willingness to arm anyone able to pay with persuasive skills endangered society. He scorned rhetorical brilliance as "the semblance of politics" in *Gorgias*. Of course, Socrates was no mean orator himself, and his deceptive denial and reliance on manipulative language provides a paradigm for all political debate. While at one moment rejecting fancy and delusory talk, Mario Cuomo went on to create his own artistic vision of America, and even as he tried to dispel the "clouds" of Democratic speeches, President Reagan created his own castles in the sky.

We should distrust language. Ironically, even when our access to information about the country and the world is reaching levels undreamed of by previous generations, so is our susceptibility to persuasion. With more tools of marketing at their disposal than ever before, politicians in the television age can hide almost entirely behind pictures and words, presenting themselves—and us—in whatever costumes and masks various "communication experts" prescribe. This kind of rhetoric threatens to leave us with nothing but "the semblance of politics." Two days after his defeat, Walter Mondale reflected on the past and coming elections with much more candor than we saw on either side during the campaign:

> Modern politics today requires a mastery of television. . . . The thing that scares me about that [is] American politics is losing its substance. It is losing the debate on merit. It's losing the depth, that tough problems require discussion. More and more it is these 20-second snippets.
>
> I hope we don't lose in America this demand that those of us who want this office must be serious people of substance and depth and must be prepared not to handle the 10-second gimmick that deals, say, with little things like war and peace.[3]

The long campaign of 1984 offered some hopeful signs along with ill omens for our rhetorical prospects. Mondale's line, "Where's the beef?" effectively helped to pierce the vague promise of Gary Hart's "new ideas," and Geraldine Ferraro's at times casual and even careless remarks bespoke a resistance to the laws of prepackaged rhetoric dictated by image consultants. Nevertheless, these few bright spots were themselves cynical manipulations of symbols at another level. The task facing us as citizens, as readers of political communication, is the development of a perpetually vigilant skepticism, of new skills in questioning and analyzing, and of doubt and disbelief. President Reagan's constant efforts to make us believe in America, in ourselves as he describes us, are two-sided achievements. On the one hand, he has given many Americans a new sense of national pride. But on the other, Reagan's rhetoric has appealed to and encouraged one of our worst habits, the desire to believe which goes beyond even gullibility. As we gear up for the next presidential campaign, both major parties seem to hope for another great communicator to duplicate Ronald Reagan's power to move voters with words. This trend should distress us, for the use of language requires not only the ability to speak or write, but also the skill of questioning the words we hear. We need to listen more suspiciously not simply to avoid being duped by a potential tyrant or an incompetent leader of any political persuasion, but also to keep us from becoming deaf and blind to our own cultural language. Such scrutiny is the first duty of democracy.

NOTES

1. *Newsweek: Election Extra:* AVALANCHE, Vol. CIV, Number 21 (November/December 1984), p. 82.
2. George Orwell, "Politics and the English Language," *Shooting an Elephant* (New York: Harcourt, Brace and Company, 1945), p. 92.
3. Bernard Weinraub, "Mondale Farewell," *The New York Times,* November 8, 1984, pp. A–1, A–24.

APPENDIX / SELECTED SPEECHES OF RONALD REAGAN

"A *Time for Choosing*," October 27, 1964

I am going to talk of controversial things. I make no apology for this. I have been talking on this subject for ten years, obviously under the administration of both parties. I mention this only because it seems impossible to legitimately debate the issues of the day without being subjected to name-calling and the application of labels. Those who deplore the use of the terms "pink" and "leftist" are themselves guilty of branding all who oppose their liberalism as right wing extremists. How long can we afford the luxury of this family fight when we are at war with the most dangerous enemy ever known to man?

If we lose that war, and in so doing lose our freedom, it has been said history will record with the greatest astonishment that those who had the most to lose did the least to prevent its happening. The guns are silent in this war but frontiers fall while those who should be warriors prefer neutrality. Not long age two friends of mine were talking to a Cuban refugee. He was a businessman who had escaped from Castro. In the midst of his tale of horrible experiences, one of my friends turned to the other and said, "We don't know how lucky we are." The Cuban stopped and said, "How lucky you are? I had some place to escape to." And in that sentence he told the entire story. If freedom is lost here there is no place to escape to.

It's time we asked ourselves if we still know the freedoms intended for us by the Founding Fathers. James Madison said, "We base all our experiments on the capacity of mankind for self-government." This idea that government was beholden to the people, that it had no other source of power except that sovereign people, is still the newest, most unique idea in all the long history of man's relation to man. For almost two centuries we have provided man's capacity for self-government, but today we are told we must choose between a left and a right or, as others suggest, a third alternative, a kind of safe middle ground. I suggest to you there is no left or right, only an up or down. Up to the maximum of individual freedom consistent with law and order, or down to the ant heap of totalitarianism; and regardless of their humanitarian purpose those who would sacrifice freedom for security have, whether they know it or not, chosen this downward path. Plutarch warned, "The real destroyer of the liberties of the people is he who spreads among them bounties, donations, and benefits."

Today there is an increasing number who can't see a fat man standing beside a thin one without automatically coming to the conclusion the fat one got that way by taking advantage of the thin one. So they would seek the answer to all the problems of human need through government. Howard K. Smith of television fame has written, "The profit motive is outmoded. It must be replaced by the incentives of the welfare state." He says, "The distribution of goods must be effected by a planned economy."

Another articulate spokesman for the welfare state defines liberalism as meeting the material needs of the masses through the full power of centralized government. I for one find it disturbing when a representative refers to the free men and women of this country as the masses, but beyond this the full power of centralized government was the very thing the Founding Fathers sought to minimize. They knew you don't control things; you can't control the economy without controlling *people*. So we have come to a time for choosing. Either we accept the responsibility for our own destiny, or we abandon the American Revolution and confess that an intellectual belief in a far-distant capitol can plan our lives for us better than we can plan them ourselves.

Already the hour is late. Government has laid its hand on health, housing, farming, industry, commerce, education, and, to an ever-increasing degree, interferes with the people's right to know. Government tends to grow; government programs take on weight and momentum, as public servants say, always with the best of intentions, "What greater service we could render if only we had a little more money and a little more power." But the truth is that outside of its legitimate function, government does nothing as well or as economically as the private sector of the economy. What better example do we have of this than government's involvement in the farm economy over the last thirty years. One-fourth of farming has seen a steady decline in the per capita consumption of everything it produces. That one-fourth is regulated and subsidized by government.

In contrast, the three-fourths of farming unregulated and unsubsidized has seen a 21 percent increase in the per capita consumption of all its produce. Since 1955 the cost of the farm program has nearly doubled. Direct payment to farmers is eight times as great as it was nine years ago, but farm income remains unchanged while farm surplus is bigger. In that same period we have seen a decline of five million in the farm population, but an increase in the number of Department of Agriculture employees.

There is now one such employee for every thirty farms in the United States, and still they can't figure how sixty-six shiploads of grain headed for Austria could disappear without a trace, and Billy Sol Estes never left shore. Three years ago the government put into effect a program to curb the over-production of feed gain. Now, $2.5 billion later, the corn crop is one hundred million bushels bigger than before the program started. And the cost of the program prorates out to $43 for every dollar bushel of corn we don't grow. Nor is this the only example of the price we pay for government meddling. Some government programs with the passage of time take on a sacrosanct quality.

One such considered above criticism, sacred as motherhood, is TVA. This program started as a flood control project; the Tennessee Valley was periodically ravaged by destructive floods. The Army Engineers set out to solve this problem. They said that it was possible that once in 500 years there could be a total capacity flood that would inundate some six hundred thousand acres. Well, the engineers fixed that. They made a permanent lake which inundated a million acres. This solved the problem of floods, but the annual interest on the TVA debt is five times as large as the annual flood damage they sought to correct.

Of course, you will point out that TVA gets electric power from the impounded waters, and this is true, but today 85 percent of TVA's electricity is generated in the coal-burning steam plants. Now perhaps you'll charge that I'm overlooking the navigable waterway that was created, providing cheap barge traffic, but the bulk of the freight barged on that waterway is coal being shipped to the TVA steam plants, and the cost of maintaining that channel each year would pay for shipping all of the coal by rail, and there would be money left over.

One last argument remains: the prosperity produced by such

large programs of government spending. Certainly there are few areas where more spending has taken place. The Labor Department lists 50 percent of the 169 counties in the Tennessee Valley as permanent areas of poverty, distress, and unemployment.

Meanwhile, back in the city, under Urban Renewal, the assault on freedom carries on. Private property rights have become so diluted that public interest is anything a few planners decide it should be. In Cleveland, Ohio, to get a project under way, city officials reclassified eighty-four buildings as substandard in spite of the fact their own inspectors had previously pronounced these buildings sound. The owners stood by and watched 26 million dollars worth of property as it was destroyed by the headache ball. Senate Bill 628 says, "Any property, be it home or commercial structure, can be declared slum or blighted and the owner has no recourse at law. The Law Division of the Library of Congress and the General Accounting Office have said that the Courts will have to rule against the owner."

Housing. In one key Eastern city a man owning a blighted area sold his property to Urban Renewal for several million dollars. At the same time, he submitted his own plan for the rebuilding of this area and the government sold him back his own property for 22 percent of what they paid. Now the government announces, "We are going to build subsidized housing in the thousands where we have been building in the hundreds." At the same time FHA and the Veterans Administration reveal they are holding 120 thousand housing units reclaimed from mortgage foreclosure, mostly because the low down payment and the easy terms brought the owners to a point where they realized the unpaid balance on the homes amounted to a sum greater than the homes were worth, so they just walked out the front door, possibly to take up residence in newer subsidized housing, again with little or no down payment and easy terms.

Some of the foreclosed homes had already been bulldozed into the earth, others, it has been announced, will be refurbished and put on sale for down payments as low as $100 and thirty-five years to pay. This will give the bulldozers a second crack. It is in the area of social welfare that government has found its most fertile growing bed. So many of us accept our responsibility for those less fortunate. We are susceptible to humanitarian appeals.

Federal welfare spending is today ten times greater than it was in the dark depths of the Depression. Federal, state, and local welfare combined spend 45 billion dollars a year. Now the government has announced that 20 percent, some 9.3 million families, are poverty stricken on the basis that they have less than a $3,000 a year income.

If this present welfare spending was prorated equally among these poverty-stricken families, we could give each family more than $4,500 a year. Actually, direct aid to the poor averages less than $600 per family. There must be some administrative overhead somewhere. Now, are we to believe that another billion dollar program added to the half a hundred programs and the 45 billion dollars, will, through some magic, end poverty? For three decades we have tried to solve unemployment by government planning, without success. The more the plans fail, the more the planners plan.

The latest is the Area Redevelopment Agency, and in two years less than one-half of one percent of the unemployed could attribute new jobs to this agency, and the cost to the taxpayer for each job found was $5,000. But beyond the great bureaucratic waste, what are we doing to the people we seek to help?

Recently a judge told me of an incident in his court. A fairly young woman with six children, pregnant with her seventh, came to him for a divorce. Under his questioning it became apparent her husband did not share this desire. Then the whole story came out. Her husband was a laborer earning $250 a month. By divorcing him she could get an $80 raise. She was eligible for $350 a month from the Aid to Dependent Children

Program. She had been talked into this divorce by two friends who had already done this very thing. But any time we question the schemes of the dogooders, we are denounced as being opposed to their humanitarian goal. It seems impossible to legitimately debate their solutions with the assumption that all of us share the desire to help those less fortunate. They tell us we are always against, never for anything. Well, it isn't so much that liberals are ignorant. It's just that they know so much that isn't so.

We are for a provision that destitution should not follow unemployment by reason of old age. For that reason we have accepted Social Security as a step toward meeting that problem. However, we are against the irresponsibility of those who charge that any criticism or suggested improvement of the program means we want to end payment to those who depend on Social Security for a livelihood.

Fiscal Irresponsibility. We have been told in millions of pieces of literature and press releases that Social Security is an insurance program, but the executives of Social Security appeared before the Supreme Court in the case of *Nestor* vs. *Fleming* and proved to the Court's satisfaction that it is not insurance but is a welfare program, and Social Security dues are a tax for the general use of the government. Well it can't be both: insurance and welfare. Later, appearing before a Congressional Committee, they admited that Social Security is today 28 billion dollars in the red. This fiscal irresponsibility has already caught up with us.

Faced with a bankruptcy, we find today that a young man in his early twenties, going to work at less than an average salary, will, with his employer, pay into Social Security an amount which could provide the young man with a retirement insurance policy guranteeing $220 a month at age 65, and the government promises him $127.

Now, are we so lacking in business sense that we cannot put this program on a sound actuarial basis, so that those who do depend on it won't come to the cupboard and find it bare, and at the same time can't we introduce voluntary features so that those who can make better provision for themselves are allowed to do so? Incidentally, we might also allow participants in Social Security to name their own beneficiaries, which they cannot do in the present program. These are not insurmountable problems.

Youth Aid Plans. We have today 30 million workers protected by industrial and union pension funds that are soundly financed by some 70 billion dollars invested in corporate securities and income earning real estate. I think we are for telling our senior citizens that no one in this country should be denied medical care for lack of funds, but we are against forcing all citizens into a compulsory government program regardless of need. Now the government has turned its attention to our young people, and suggests that it can solve the problem of school dropouts and juvenile delinquency through some kind of revival of the old C.C.C. camps. The suggested plan prorates out to a cost of $4,700 a year for each young person we want to help. We can send them to Harvard for $2,700 a year. Of course, don't get me wrong—I'm not suggesting Harvard as the answer to juvenile delinquency.

We are for an international organization where the nations of the world can legitimately seek peace. We are against subordinating American interests to an organization so structurally unsound that a two-thirds majority can be mustered in the U.N. General Assembly among nations representing less than 10 percent of the world population.

Is there not something of hypocrisy in assailing our allies for so-called vestiges of colonialism while we engage in a conspiracy of silence about the peoples enslaved by the Soviet in the satellite nations? We are for aiding our allies by sharing our material blessings with those nations which share our fundamental beliefs. We are against doling out money, government to government, which ends up financing socialism all over the world.

We set out to help nineteen war-ravaged countries at the end of

World War II. We are now helping 107. We have spent 146 billion dollars. Some of that money bought a $2 million yacht for Haile Selassie. We bought dress suits for Greek undertakers. We bought one thousand TV sets with 23-inch screens for a country where there is no electricity, and some of our foreign aid funds provided extra wives for Kenya government officials. When Congress moved to cut foreign aid they were told that if they cut it one dollar they endangered national security, and then Senator Harry Byrd revealed that since its inception foreign aid has rarely spent its alloted budget. It has today $21 billion in unexpended funds.

Some time ago Dr. Howard Kershner was speaking to the Prime Minister of Lebanon. The Prime Minister told him proudly that his little country balanced its budget each year. It had no public debt, no inflation, a modest tax rate, and had increased its gold holdings from seventy to 120 million dollars. When he finished, Dr. Kershner said, "Mr. Prime Minister, my country hasn't balanced its budget twenty-eight out of the last forty years. My country's debt is bigger than the combined debt of all the nations of the world. We have inflation, we have a tax rate that takes from the private sector a percentage of income greater than any civilized nation has ever taken and survived. We have lost gold at such a rate that the solvency of our currency is in danger. Do you think that my country should continue to give your country millions of dollars each year?" The Prime Minister smiled and said, "no, but if you are foolish enough to do it, we are going to keep on taking the money."

Nine Stalls For One Bull. And so we built a model stock farm in Lebanon, and we built nine stalls for each bull. I find something peculiarly appropriate in that. We have in our vaults $15 billion in gold. We don't own an ounce. Foreign claims against that gold total $27 billion. In the last six years, fifty-two nations have bought $7 billion worth of our gold and all fifty-two are receiving foreign aid.

Because no government ever voluntarily reduces itself in size, government programs once launched never go out of existence. A government agency is the nearest thing to eternal life we'll ever see on this earth. The United States Manual takes twenty-five pages to list by name every Congressman and Senator, and all the agencies controlled by Congress. It then lists the agencies coming under the Executive Branch, and this requires 520 pages.

Since the beginning of the century our gross national product has increased by thirty-three times. In the same period the cost of federal government has increased 234 times, and while the work force is only one and one-half times greater, federal employees number nine times as many. There are now two and one-half million federal employees. No one knows what they all do. One Congressman found out what one of them does. This man sits at a desk in Washington. Documents come to him each morning. He reads them, initials them, and passes them on to the proper agency. One day a document arrived he wasn't supposed to read, but he read it, initialled it and passed it on. Twenty-four hours later it arrived back at his desk with a memo attached that said, "You weren't supposed to read this. Erase your initials, and initial the erasure."

While the federal government is the great offender, the idea filters down. During a period in California when our population has increased 90 percent, the cost of state government has gone up 862 percent and the number of employees 500 percent. Governments, state and local, now employ one out of six of the nation's work force. If the rate of increase of the last three years continues, by 1970 one-fourth of the total work force will be employed by government. Already we have a permanent structure so big and complex it is virtually beyond the control of Congress and the comprehension of the people, and tyranny inevitably follows when this permanent structure usurps the policy-making function that belongs to elected officials.

One example of this occurred when Congress was debating

whether to lend the United Nations $100 million. While they debated, the State Department gave the United Nations $217 million and the United Nations used part of that money to pay the delinquent dues of Castro's Cuba.

Under bureaucratic regulations adopted with no regard to the wish of the people, we have lost much of our Constitutional freedom. For example, federal agents can invade a man's property without a warrent, can impose a fine without a formal hearing, let alone a trial by jury, and can seize and sell his property at auction to enforce payment of that fine.

Rights by Dispensation. An Ohio deputy fire marshal sentenced a man to prison after a secret proceeding in which the accused was not allowed to have a lawyer present. The Supreme Court upheld that sentence, ruling that it was an administrative investigation of incidents damaging to the economy. Some place a perversion has taken place. Our natural unalienable rights are now presumed to be a dispensation of government, divisible by a vote of the majority. The greatest good for the greatest number is a high-sounding phrase but contrary to the very basis of our nation, unless it is accompanied by recognition that we have certain rights which cannot be infringed upon, even if the individual stands outvoted by all of his fellow citizens. Without this recognition, majority rule is nothing more than mob rule.

It is time we realize that socialism can come without overt seizure of property or nationalization of private business. It matters little that you hold the title to your property or business if government can dictate policy and procedure and holds life and death power over your business. The machinery of this power already exists. Lowell Mason, former antitrust law enforcer for the Federal Trade Commission, has written "American business is being harassed, bled and even blackjacked under a preposterous crazy quilt system of laws." There are so many that the government literally can find some charge to bring against any concern it chooses to prosecute. Are we safe in our books and records?

The natural gas producers have just been handed a 428-page questionnaire by the Federal Power Commission. It weighs ten pounds. One firm has estimated it will take 70,000 accountant manhours to fill out this questionnaire, and it must be done in quadruplicate. The Power Commission says it must have it to determine whether a proper price is being charged for gas. The National Labor Relations Board ruled that a business firm could not discontinue its shipping department even though it was more efficient and economical to subcontract this work out.

The Supreme Court has ruled the government has the right to tell a citizen what he can grow on his own land for his own use. The Secretary of Agriculture has asked for the right to imprison farmers who violate their planting quotas. One business firm has been informed by the Internal Revenue Service that it cannot take a tax deduction for its institutional advertising because this advertising espoused views not in the public interest.

A child's prayer in a school cafeteria endangers religious freedom, but the people of the Amish religion in the State of Ohio, who cannot participate in Social Security because of their religious beliefs, have had their livestock seized and sold at auction to enforce payment of Social Security dues.

We approach a point of no return when government becomes so huge and entrenched that we fear the consequences of upheaval and just go along with it. The federal government accounts for one-fifth of the industrial capacity of the nation, one-fourth of all construction, holds or guarantees one-third of all mortgages, owns, one-third of the land, and engages in some nineteen thousand businesses covering half a hundred different lines. The Defense Department runs 269 supermarkets. They do a gross business of $730 million a year, and lose $150 million. The government spends $11 million an hour every hour of the twenty-four and pretends we had a tax cut while it pursues a policy of planned inflation that will more than wipe out any benefit with depreciation of our purchasing power.

We need true tax reform that will at least make a start toward restoring for our children the American dream that wealth is denied to no one, that each individual has the right to fly as high as his strength and ability will take him. The economist Summer Schlicter has said, "If a visitor from Mars looked at our tax policy, he would conclude it had been designed by a Communist spy to make free enterprise unworkable." But we cannot have such reform while our tax policy is engineered by people who view the tax as a means of achieving changes in our social structure. Senator [Joseph S.] Clark (D.-Pa.) says the tax issue is a class issue, and the government must use the tax to redistribute the wealth and earnings downward.

Karl Marx. On January 15th in the White House, the President [Lyndon Johnson] told the group of citizens they were going to take all the money they thought was being unnecessarily spent, "take it from the haves and gives it to the have-nots who need it so much." When Karl Marx said this he put it: . . . "from each according to his ability, to each according to his need."

Have we the courage and the will to face up to the immorality and discrimination of the progressive surtax, and demand a return to traditional proportionate taxation? Many decades ago the Scottish economist, John Ramsey McCulloch, said, "The moment you abandon the cardinal principle of exacting from all individuals the same proportion of their income or their property, you are at sea without a rudder or compass and there is no amount of injustice or folly you may not commit."

No nation has survived the tax burden that reached one-third of its national income. Today in our country the tax collector's share is thirty-seven cents of every dollar earned. Freedom has never been so fragile, so close to slipping from our grasp. I wish I could give you some magic formula, but each of us must find his own role. One man in Virginia found what he could do, and dozens of business firms have followed his lead. Concerned because his two hundred employees seemed unworried about government extravagence he conceived idea of taking all of their withholding out of only the fourth paycheck each month. For three paydays his employees received their full salary. On the fourth payday all withholding was taken. He has one employee who owes him $4.70 each fourth payday. It took one month to produce two hundred conservatives.

Are you willing to spend time studying the issues, making yourself aware, and then conveying that information to family and friends? Will you resist the temptation to get a government handout for your community? Realize that the doctor's fight against socialized medicine is your fight. We can't socialize the doctors without socializing the patient. Recognize that government invasion of public power is eventually an assault upon your own business. If some among you fear taking a stand because you are afraid of reprisals from customers, clients, or even government, recognize that you are just feeding the crocodile hoping he'll eat you last.

If all of this seems like a great deal of trouble, think what's at stake. We are faced with the most evil enemy mankind has known in his long climb from the swamp to the stars. There can be no security anywhere in the free world if there is not fiscal and economic stability within the United States. Those who ask us to trade our freedom for the soup kitchen of the welfare state are architects of a policy of accomodation. They tell us that by avoiding a direct confrontation with the enemy he will learn to love us and give up his evil ways. All who oppose this idea are blanket indicted as war-monger. Well, let us set one thing straight, there is no argument with regard to peace and war. It is cheap demagoguery to suggest that anyone would want to send other people's sons to war. The only argument is with regard to the best way to avoid war. There is only one sure way—surrender.

Appeasement or Courage? The spectre our well-meaning liberal friends refuse to face is that their policy of accomodation is appeasment, and appeasement does not give you a choice between peace and war, only between fight and surrender. We are told that the problem is too complex for a simple answer. They are wrong. There is no easy answer, but there is a simple answer. We must have the courage to do what we know is morally right, and this policy of accomodation asks us to accept the greatest possible immorality. We are being asked to buy our safety from the threat of "the bomb" by selling into permanent slavery our fellow human beings enslaved behind the Iron Curtain, to tell them to give up their hope of freedom because we are ready to make a deal with their slave masters.

Alexander Hamilton warned us that a nation which can prefer disgrace to danger is prepared for a master and deserves one. Admittedly there is a risk in any course we follow. Choosing the high road cannot eliminate that risk. Already some of the architects of accommodation have hinted what their decision will be if their plan fails and we are faced with the final ultimatum. The English commentator [Kenneth] Tynan has put it this way: he would rather live on his knees than die on his feet. Some of our own have said "Better Red than dead." If we are to believe that nothing is worth the dying, when did this begin? Should Moses have told the children of Israel to live in slavery rather than dare the wilderness? Should Christ have refused the Cross? Should the patriots at Concord Bridge have refused to fire the shot heard 'round the world? Are we to believe that all the martyrs of history died in vain?

You and I have a rendezvous with destiny. We can preserve for our children this, the last best hope of man on earth, or we can sentence them to take the first step into a thousand years of darkness. If we fail, at least let our children and our children's children say of us we justified our brief moment here. We did all that could be done.

"Inaugural Address of President Ronald Reagan," January 20, 1981.

To a few of us here today this is a solemn and most momentous occasion. And, yet, in the history of our nation it is a commonplace occurence. The orderly transfer of authority as called for in the Constitution routinely takes place, as it has for almost two centuries, and few of us stop to think how unique we really are. In the eyes of many in the world, this every-four-year ceremony we accept as normal is nothing less than a miracle.

Mr. President, I want our fellow citizens to know how much you did to carry on this tradition. By your gracious cooperation in the transition process you have shown a watching world that we are a united people pledged to maintaining a political system which guarantees individual liberty to a greater degree than any other. And I thank you and your people for all the help in maintaining the continuity which is the bulwark of our Republic.

The business of our nation goes forward. These United States are confronted with an economic affliction of great proportions. We suffer from the longest and one of the worst sustained inflations in our national history. It distorts our economic decisions, penalizes thrift, and crushes the struggling young and the fixed-income elderly alike. It threatens to shatter the lives of millions of our people.

Idle industries have cast workers into unemployment, human misery, and personal indignity. Those who do work are denied a fair return for their labor by a tax system which penalizes successful achievement and keeps us from maintaining full productivity.

But great as our tax burden is, it has not kept pace with public spending. For decades we have piled deficit upon deficit, mortgaging our future and our children's future for the temporary convenience of the present. To continue this long trend is to guarantee tremendous social, cultural, political, and economic upheavals.

You and I, as individuals, can, by borrowing, live beyond our means, but for only a limited period of time. Why then, should we think that collectively, as a nation, we're not bound by that same limitation? We must act today in order to preserve tomorrow. And let there be no misunderstanding—we are going to begin to act, beginning today.

The economic ills we suffer have come upon us over several decades. They will not go away in days, weeks, or months, but they will go away. They will go away because we as Americans have the capacity now, as we've had in the past, to do whatever needs to be done to preserve this last and great bastion of freedom.

In this present crisis, government is not the solution to our problem; government *is* the problem. From time to time we've been tempted to believe that society has become too complex to be managed by self-rule, that government by an elite group is superior to government for, by, and of the people. But if no one among us is capable of governing himself, then who among us has the capacity to govern someone else? All of us together—in and out of government—must bear the burden. The solutions we seek must be equitable with no one group singled out to pay a higher price.

We hear much of special interest groups. Well, our concern must be for a special interest group that has been too long neglected. It knows no sectional boundaries or ethnic and racial divisions, and it crosses political party lines. It is made up of men and women who raise our food, patrol our streets, man our mines and factories, teach our children, keep our homes, and heal us when we're sick—professionals, industrialists, shopkeepers, clerks, cabbies, and truckdrivers. They are, in short, "We the people"—this breed called Americans.

Well, this administration's objective will be a healthy, vigorous, growing economy that provides equal opportunities for all Americans with no barriers born of bigotry or discrimination. Putting America back to work means putting all Americans back to work. Ending inflation means freeing all Americans from the terror of runaway living costs. All must share in the productive work of this "new beginning," and all must share in the bounty of a revived economy. With the idealism and fair play which are the core of our system and our strength, we can have a strong and prosperous America at peace with itself and the world.

So, as we begin, let us take inventory. We are a nation that has a government—not the other way around. And this makes us special among the nations of the Earth. Our government has no power except that granted it by the people. It is time to check and reverse the growth of government which shows signs of having grown beyond the consent of the governed.

It is my intention to curb the size and influence of the federal establishment and to demand recognition of the distinction between the powers granted to the federal government and those reserved to the states or to the people. All of us—all of us need to be reminded that the federal government did not create the states; the states created the federal government.

Now, so there will be no misunderstanding, it is not my intention to do away with the government. It is rather to make it work—work with us, not over us; to stand by our side, not ride on our back. Government can and must provide opportunity, not smother it; foster productivity, not stifle it.

If we look to the answer as to why for so many years we achieved so much, prospered as no other people on Earth, it was because here in this land we unleashed the energy and individual genius of man to a greater extent that has ever been done before. Freedom and the dignity of the individual have been more available and assured here than in any other place on Earth. The price for this freedom at times has been high. But we have never been unwilling to pay that price.

It is no coincidence that our present troubles parallel and are proportionate to the intervention and intrusion in our lives that result from unnecessary and excessive growth of government. It is time for us to realize that we're too great a nation to limit ourselves to small dreams. We're not, as some would have us believe, doomed to an inevitable decline. I do not believe in a fate that will fall on us no matter what we do. I do believe in a fate that will fall on us if we do nothing. So, with all the creative energy at our command, let us begin an era of national renewal. Let us renew our determination, our courage, and our strength. And let us renew our faith and our hope.

We have every right to dream heroic dreams. Those who say that we're in a time when there are no heroes, they just don't know where to look. You can see heroes every day going in and out of factory gates. Others, a handful in number, produce enough food to feed all of us and then the world beyond. You meet heroes across a counter. And they're on both sides of that counter. There are entrepreneurs with faith in themselves and faith in an idea, who create new jobs, new wealth and opportunity. There are individuals and families whose taxes support the government and whose voluntary gifts support church, charity, culture, art, and education. Their patriotism is quiet but deep. Their values sustain our national life.

Now, I have used the words, "they" and "their" in speaking of these heroes. I could say "you" and "your," because I'm addressing the heroes of whom I speak—you, the citizens of this blessed land. Your dreams, your hopes, your goals are going to be the dreams, the hopes and the goals of this administration, so help me God.

We shall reflect the compassion that is so much a part of your makeup. How can we love our country and not love our countrymen; and loving them, reach out a hand when they fall, heal them when they're sick, and provide opportunity to make them self-sufficient so they will be equal in fact and not just in theory?

Can we solve the problems confronting us? Well, the answer is an unequivocal and emphatic "yes." To paraphrase Winston Churchill, I did not take the oath I've just taken with the intention of presiding over the dissolution of the world's strongest economy.

In the days ahead I will propose removing the roadblocks that have slowed our economy and reduced productivity. Steps will be taken aimed at restoring the balance between the various levels of government. Progress may be slow—measured in inches and feet, not miles—but we will progress. It is time to reawaken this industrial giant, to get government back within its means, and to lighen our punitive tax burden. And these will be our first priorities, and on these principles there will be no compromise.

On the eve of our struggle for independence a man who might have been one of the greatest among the Founding Fathers, Dr. Joseph Warren, president of the Massachusetts Congress, said to his fellow Americans, "Our country is in danger, but not to be despaired of. On you depend the fortunes of America. You are to decide the important question upon which rests the happiness and the liberty of millions yet unborn. Act worthy of yourselves."

Well, I believe we, the Americans of today, are ready to act worthy of ourselves, ready to do what must be done to ensure happiness and liberty for ourselves, our children, and our children's children. And as we renew ourselves here in our own land, we will be seen as having greater strength throughout the world. We will again be the exemplar of freedom and a beacon of hope for those who do not now have freedom.

To those neighbors and allies who share our freedom, we will strengthen our historic ties and assure them of our support and firm commitment. We will match loyalty with loyalty. We will strive for mutually beneficial relations. We will not use our friendship to impose on their sovereignty, for our own sovereignty is not for sale.

As for enemies of freedom, those who are potential adversaries, they will be reminded that peace is the highest aspiration of the American people. We will negotiate for it, sacrifice for it; we will not surrender for it—now or ever.

Our forbearance should never be misunderstood. Our reluctance for conflict should not be misjudged as a failure of will. When action is required to preserve our national security, we will act. We will maintain sufficient strength to prevail if need be, knowing that if we do, we have the best chance of never having to use that strength.

Above all, we must realize that no arsenal or no weapon in the arsenals of the world is so formidable as the will and moral courage of free men and women. It is a weapon our adversaries in today's world do not have. It is a weapon that we as Americans do have. Let that be understood by those who practice terrorism and prey upon their neighbors.

I am told that tens of thousands of prayer meetings are being held on this day; for that I'm deeply grateful. We are a nation under God, and I believe God intended for us to be free. It would be fitting and good, I think, if on each Inaugural Day in future years, there should be declared a day of prayer.

This is the first time in our history that this ceremony has been held, as you've been told, on this West Front of the Capitol. Standing here, one faces a magnificent vista, opening up on this city's special beauty and history. At the end of this open mall are those shrines to the giants on whose shoulders we stand.

Directly in front of me, the monument to a monumental man, George Washington, father of our country. A man of humility who came to greatness reluctantly. He led America out of revolutionary victory into infant nationhood. Off to one side, the stately memorial to Thomas Jefferson. The Declaration of Independence flames with his eloquence. And then, beyond the Reflecting Pool, the dignified columns of the Lincoln Memorial. Whoever would understand in his heart the meaning of America will find it in the life of Abraham Lincoln.

Beyond those monuments of heroism is the Potomac River, and on the far shore the sloping hills of Arlington National Cemetary, with its row upon row of simple white markers bearing crosses or Stars of David. They add up to only a tiny fraction of the price that has been paid for our freedom.

One such marker is a monument to the kind of hero I spoke of earlier. Their lives ended in places called Belleau Wood, The Argonne, Omaha Beach, Salerno, and halfway around the world on Guadalcanal, Tarawa, Pork Chop Hill, the Chosin Reservoir, and in a hundred rice paddies and jungles of a place called Vietnam.

Under one such marker lies a young man, Martin Treptow, who left his job in a small town barbershop in 1917 to go to France with the famed Rainbow Division. There, on the Western Front, he was killed trying to carry a message between battalions under heavy artillery fire.

We're told that on his body was found a diary. On the flyleaf under the heading, "My Pledge," he had written these words: "America must win this war. Therefore I will work, I will save, I will sacrifice, I will endure, I will fight cheerfully and do my utmost, as if the issue of the whole struggle depended on me alone."

The crisis we are facing today does not require of us the kind of sacrifice that Martin Treptow and so many thousands of others were called upon to make. It does require, however, our best effort and our willingness to believe in ourselves and to believe in our capacity to perform great deeds; to believe that together with God's help we can and will resolve the problems which now confront us.

And, after all, why shouldn't we believe that? We are Americans.

God bless you and thank you.

"University of Notre Dame: Address at Commencement Exercises at the University," May 17, 1981

Father Hesburgh, I thank you very much and for so many things. The distinguished honor that you're conferred upon me here today, I must say, however, compounds a sense of guilt that I have nursed for almost 50 years. I thought the first degree I was given was honorary. But it's wonderful to be here today with Governor Orr, Governor Bowen, Senators Lugar and Quayle, and Representative Hiler, these distinguished honorees, the trustees, administration, faculty, students, and friends of Notre Dame and most important, the graduating class of 1981.

Nancy and I are greatly honored to share this day with you, and our pleasure has been more than doubled because I am also sharing the platform with a longtime and very dear friend, Pat O'Brien.

Pat and I haven't been able to see much of each other lately, so I haven't had a chance to tell him that there is now another tie that binds us together. Until a few weeks ago I knew very little about our father's ancestry. He had been orphaned at age 6. But now I've learned that his grandfather, my great-grandfather, left Ireland to come to America, leaving his home in Ballyporeen, a village in County Tipperary in Ireland, and I have learned that Ballyporeen is the ancestral home of the O'Brien's.

Now, if I don't watch out, this may turn out to be less of a commencement than a warm bath in nostalgic memories. Growing up in Illinois, I was influenced by a sports legend so national in scope, it was almost mystical. It is difficult to explain to anyone who didn't live in those times. The legend was based on a combination of three elements: a game, football; a university, Notre Dame; and a man, Knute Rockne. There has been nothing like it before or since.

My first time to ever see Notre Dame was to come here as a sports announcer 2 years out of college, to broadcast a football game. You won or I wouldn't have mentioned it.

A number of years later I returned here in the company of Pat O'Brien and a galaxy of Hollywood stars for the world premier of "Knute Rockne—All American" in which I was privileged to play George Gipp. I've always suspected that there might have been many actors in Hollywood who could have played the part better, but no one could have wanted to play it more than I did. And I was given the part largely because the star of that picture, Pat O'Brien, kindly and generously held out a helping hand to a beginning young actor.

Having come from the world of sports, I'd been trying to write a story about Knute Rockne. I must confess that I had someone in mind to play the Gipper. On one of my sports broadcasts before going to Hollywood, I had told the story of his career and tragic death. I didn't have very many words on paper when I learned that the studio that employed me was already preparing a story treatment for the film. And that brings me to the theme of my remarks.

I'm the fifth President of the United States to address a Notre Dame commencement. The temptation is great to use this forum as an address on a great international or national issue that has nothing to do with this occasion. Indeed, this is somewhat traditional. So, I wasn't surprised when I read in several reputable journals that I was going to deliver an address on foreign policy or on the economy. I'm not going to talk about either.

But, by the same token, I'll try not to belabor you with some of the standard rhetoric that is beloved of graduation speakers. For example, I'm not going to tell you that "You know more today than you've ever known before or that you will ever know again." The other standby is, "When I was 14, I didn't think my father knew anything. By the time I was 21, I was amazed at how much the old gentleman had learned in 7 years." And then, of course, the traditional and the standby is that "A University like this is a storehouse of knowledge because the freshmen bring so much in and the seniors take so little away."

You members of the class of 18—or 1981—I don't really go back that far—are what behaviorists call achievers. And while you will look back with warm pleasure on your memories of these years that brought you here to where you are today, you are also, I know, looking at the future that seems uncertain to most of you but which, let me assure you, offers great expectations.

Take pride in this day. Thank your parents, as one on your behalf has already done here. Thank those who've been of help to you over the last 4 years. And do a little celebrating; you're entitled. This is your day, and whatever I say should take cognizance of that fact. It is a milestone in life, and it marks a time of change.

Winston Churchill, during the darkest period of the "Battle of Britain" in World War II said: "When great causes are on the move in the world . . . we learn we are spirits, not animals, and that something is going on in space and time, and beyond space and time, whether we like it or not, spells duty."

Now, I'm going to mention again that movie that Pat and I and Notre Dame were in, because it says something about America. First, Knute Rockne as a boy came to America with his parents from Norway. And in the few years it took him to grow up to college age, he became so American that here at Notre Dame, he became an All American in a game that is still, to this day, uniquely American.

As a coach, he did more than teach young men how to play a game. He believed truly that the noblest work of man was building the character of man. And maybe that's why he was a living legend. No man connected with football has ever achieved the stature or occupied the singular niche in the Nation that he carved out for himself, not just in a sport, but in our entire social structure.

Now, today I hear very often, "Win one for the Gipper," spoken in a humorous vein. Lately I've been hearing it by Congressmen who are supportive of the programs that I've introduced. But let's look at the significance of that story. Rockne could have used Gipp's dying words to win a game any time. But 8 years went by following the death of George Gipp before Rock revealed those dying words, his deathbed wish.

And then he told the story at halftime to a team that was losing, and one of the only teams he had ever coached that was torn by dissention and jeolously [*sic*] and factionalism. The seniors on that team were about to close out their football careers without learning or experiencing any of the real values that a game has to impart. None of them had known George Gipp. They were children when he played for Notre Dame. It was to this team that Rockne told the story and so inspired them that they rose above their personal animosities. For someone they had never known, they joined together in a common cause and attained the unattainable.

We were told when we were making the picture of one line that was spoken by a player during the game. We were actually afraid to put it in the picture. The man who carried the ball over for the winning touchdown was injured on the play. We were told that as he was lifted on the stretcher and carried off the field he was heard to say, "That's the last one I can get for you, Gipper."

Now, it's only a game. And maybe to hear it now, afterward—and this is what we feared—it might sound maudlin and not the way it was intended. But is there anything wrong with young people having an experience, feeling something so deeply, thinking of someone else to the point that they can give so completely of themselves? There will come times in the lives of all of us when we'll be faced with causes bigger than ourselves, and they won't be on a playing field.

This Nation was born when a band of men, the Founding Fathers, a group so unique we've never seen their like since, rose to such selfless heights. Lawyers, tradesmen, merchants, farmers—56 men achieved security and standing in life but valued freedom more. They pledged their lives, their fortunes, and their sacred honor. 16 of them gave their lives. Most gave their fortunes. All preserved their sacred honor.

They gave us more than a nation. They brought to all mankind for the first time the concept that man was born free, that each of us has inalienable rights, ours by the grace of God, and that government was created by us for our convenience, having only the powers that we choose to give it. This is the heritage that you're about to claim as you come out to join the society made up of those who have preceded you by a few years, or some of us by a great many.

This experiment in man's relation to man is a few years into its third century. Saying that may make it sound quite old. But let's look at it from another viewpoint or perspective. A few years ago, someone figured out that if you could condense the entire history of life on Earth into a motion picture that would run for 24 hours a day, 365 days—maybe on leap years we could have an intermission—this idea that is the United States wouldn't appear on the screen until 3 1/2 seconds before midnight on December 31st. And in those 3 1/2 seconds not only would a new concept of society come into being, a golden hope for all mankind, but more than half the activity, economic activity in world history, would take place on this continent. Free to express their genius, individual Americans, men and women, in 3 1/2 seconds, would perform such miracles of invention, construction, and production as the world had ever seen.

As you join us out there beyond the campus, you know there are great unsolved problems. Federalism, with its built in checks and balances, has been distorted. Central Government has usurped powers that properly belong to local and State governments. And in so doing, in many ways that central Government has begun to fail to do the things that are truly the responsibility of a central government.

All of this has led to the misuse of power and preemption of the prerogatives of people and their social institutions. You are graduating from a great private, or, if you will, independent university. Not too many years ago, such schools were relatively free from government interference. In recent years, Government has spawned regulations covering virtually every facet of our lives.

The independent and church-supported colleges and universities have found themselves enmeshed in that network of regulations and the costly blizzard of paperwork that Government is demanding. Thirty-four congressional committees and almost eighty subcommittees have jurisdiction over 439 separate laws affecting education at the college level alone. Almost every aspect of campus life is now regulated—hiring, firing, promotions, physical plant, construction, recordkeeping, fundraising and, to some extent, curriculum and educational programs.

I hope when you leave this campus that you will do so with a feeling of obligation to your alma mater. She will need your help and support in the years to come. If ever the great independent colleges and universities like Notre Dame give way to and are replaced by tax-supported institutions, the struggle to preserve academic freedom will have been lost.

We're troubled today by economic stagnation, brought on by inflated currency and prohibitive taxes and burdensome regulations. The cost of stagnation in human terms, mostly among those least equipped to survive it, is cruel and inhuman.

Now, after those remarks, don't decide that you'd better turn your diploma back in so you can stay another year on the campus. I've just given you the bad news. The good news is that something is being done about all this because the people of America have said, "Enough already." You know, we who had preceded you had just gotten so busy that we let things get out of hand. We forgot that we were the keepers of the power, forgot to challenge the notion that the state is the principal vehicle of social change, forgot that millions of social interactions among free individuals and institutions can do more to foster economic and social progress than all the careful schemes of government planners.

Well, at last we're remembering, remembering that government has certain legitimate functions which it can perform very well, that it can be responsive to the people, that it can be humane and compassionate, but that when it undertakes tasks that are not its proper province, it can do none of them as well or as economically as the private sector.

For too long, government has been fixing things that aren't broken and inventing miracle cures for unknown diseases.

We need you. We need your youth. We need your strength. We need your idealism to help us make right that which is wrong. Now, I know that this period of your life, you have been and are critically looking at the mores and customs of the past and questioning their value. Every generation does that. May I suggest, don't discard the time-tested values upon which civilization was built simply because they're old? More important, don't let today's doom criers and cynics persuade you that the best is past, that from here on it's all downhill. Each generation sees farther than the generation that preceded it because it stands on the shoulders of that generation. You're going to have opportunities beyond anything that we've ever known.

The people have made it plain already. They want an end to excessive government intervention in their lives and in the economy, an end to the burdensome and unnecessary regulations and a punitive tax policy that does take "from the mouth of labor the bread it has earned." They want a government that cannot only continue to send men across the vast reaches of space and bring them safely home, but that can guarantee that you and I can walk in the park of our neighborhood after dark and get safely home. And finally, they want to know that this Nation has the ability to defend itself against those who would seek to pull it down.

And all of this, we the people can do. Indeed, a start has already been made. There's a task force under the leadership of the Vice President, George Bush, that is to look at those regulations I've spoken of. They have already identified hundreds of them that can be wiped out with no harm to the quality of life. And the cancellation of just those regulations will leave billions and billions of dollars in the hands of the people for productive enterprise and research and development and the creation of jobs.

The years ahead are great ones for this country, for the cause of freedom, and the spread of civilizations. The West won't contain communism, it will transcend communism. It won't bother to dismiss or denounce it, it will dismiss it as some bizarre chapter in human history whose last pages are even now being written.

William Faulkner, at a Nobel Prize ceremony some time back, said man "would not only [merely] endure: he will prevail" against the modern world because he will return to "the old verities and truths of the heart." And then Faulkner said of man, "He is immortal because he alone among creatures . . . has a soul, a spirit capable of compassion and sacrifice and endurance."

One can't say those words, "compassion, sacrifice, and endurance," without thinking of the irony that one who so exemplifies them, Pope John Paul II, a man of peace and goodness, an inspiration to the world, would be struck down by a bullet from a man towards whom he could only feel compassion and love. It was Pope John Paul II who warned in last year's encyclical on mercy and justice against certain economic theories that use the rhetoric of class struggle to justify injustice. He said, "In the name of an alleged justice the neighbor is sometimes destroyed, killed, deprived of liberty or stripped of fundamental human rights."

For the West, for America, the time has come to dare to show to the world that our civilized ideas, our traditions, our values, are not—like the ideology and war machine of totalitarian societies—just a facade of strength. It is time for the world to know our intellectual and spiritual values are rooted in the source of all strength, a belief in a Supreme Being, and a law higher than our own.

When it's written, history of our time won't dwell long on the hardships of the recent past. But history will ask—and our answer determine the fate of freedom for a thousand years—Did a nation born of hope lose hope? Did a people forged by courage find courage wanting? Did a generation steeled by hard war and a harsh peace forsake honor at the moment of great climactic struggle for the human spirit?

If history asks such questions, it also answers them. And the answers are to be found in the heritage left by generations of Americans before us. They stand in silent witness to what the world will soon know and history someday record: that in the third century, the American Nation came of age, affirmed its leadership of free men and women serving selflessly a vision of man with God, government for people, and humanity at peace.

A few years ago, an Australian Prime Minister, John Gorton, said, "I wonder if anybody ever thought what the situation for the comparatively small nations in the world would be if there were not in existence the United States, if there were not this giant country prepared to make so many sacrifices." This is the noble and rich heritage rooted in great civil ideas of the West, and it is yours.

My hope today is that in the years to come—and come it shall—when it's your time to explain to another generation the meaning of the past and thereby hold out to them their promise of the future, that you'll recall the truths and traditions of which we've spoken. It is these truths and traditions that define our civilization and make up our national heritage. And now, they're yours to protect and pass on.

I have one more hope for you: when you do speak to the next generation about these things, that you will always be able to speak of an America that is strong and free, to find in your hearts an unbounded pride in this much-loved country, this once and future land, this bright and hopeful nation whose generous spirit and great ideals the world still honors.

Congratulations, and God bless you.

"National Association of Evangelicals; Remarks at the Annual Convention in Orlando, Florida," March 8, 1983

Reverend clergy all, Senator Hawkins, distinguished members of the Florida congressional delegation, and all of you:

I can't tell you how you have warmed my heart with your welcome. I'm delighted to be here today.

Those of you in the National Association of Evangelicals are known for your spiritual and humanitarian work. And I would be especially remiss if I didn't discharge right now one personal debt of gratitude. Thank you for your prayers. Nancy and I have felt their presence many times in many ways. And believe me, for us they've made all the difference.

The other day in the East Room of the White House at a meeting there, someone asked me whether I was aware of all the people out there who were praying for the President. And I had to say, "Yes, I am. I've felt it. I believe in intercessionary prayer." But I couldn't help but say to that questioner after he'd asked the question that—or at least say to them that if sometimes when he was praying he got a busy signal, it was just me in there ahead of him. I think I understand how Abraham Lincoln felt when he said, "I have been driven many times to my knees by the overwhelming conviction that I had nowhere else to go."

From the joy and the good feeling of this conference, I go to a political reception. Now, I don't know why, but that bit of scheduling reminds me of a story which I'll share with you.

An evangelical minister and a politician arrived at Heaven's gate one day together. And St. Peter, after doing all the necessary formalities, took them in hand to show them where their quarters would be. And he took them to a small, single room with a bed, a chair, and a table and said this was for the clergyman. And the politician was a little worried about what might be in store for him. And he couldn't believe it then when St. Peter stopped in front of a beautiful mansion with lovely grounds, many servants, and told him that these would be his quarters.

And he couldn't help but ask, he said. "But wait, how—there's something wrong—how do I get this mansion while that good and holy man only gets a single room?" And St. Peter said, "You have to understand how things are up here. We've got thousands and thousands of clergy. You're the first politician who ever made it."

But I don't want to contribute to a stereotype. So, I'll tell you there are a great many God-fearing, dedicated, noble men and women in public life, present company included. And, yes, we need your help to keep us ever mindful of the ideas and the principles that brought us into the public arena in the first place. The basis of those ideals and principles is a commitment to freedom and personal liberty that, itself, is grounded in the much deeper realization that freedom prospers only where the blessings of God are avidly sought and humbly accepted.

The American experiment in democracy rests on this insight. Its discovery was the great triumph of our Founding Fathers, voiced by William Penn when he said: "If we will not be governed by God, we must be governed by tyrants." Explaining the inalienable rights of men, Jefferson said, "The God who gave us life, gave us liberty at the same time." And it was George Washington, who said that "of all the dispositions and habits which lead to political prosperity, religion and morality are indispensible supports."

And finally, that shrewdest of all observers of American democracy, Alexis de Tocqueville, put it eloquently after he had gone on a search for the secret of American's greatness and genius—and he said: "Not until I went into the churches of America and heard her pulpits aflame with righteousness did I understand the greatness and the genius of America. . . . America is good. And if America ever ceases to be good, America will cease to be great."

Well, I'm pleased to be here today with you who are keeping America great by keeping her good. Only through your work and prayers and those of millions of others can we hope to survive this perilous century and keep alive this experiment in liberty, this last, best hope of man.

I want you to know that this administration is motivated by a political philosophy that sees the greatness of America in you, her people, and in your families, churches, neighborhoods, communities—the institutions that foster and nourish values like concern for others and respect for the rule of law under God.

Now, I don't have to tell you that this puts us in opposition to, or at least out of step with, a prevailing attitude of many who have turned to a modern-day secularism, discarding the tried and time-tested values upon which our very civilization is based. No matter how well intentioned, their value system is radically different from that of most Americans. And while they proclaim that they're freeing us from superstitions of the past, they've taken upon themselves the job of superintending us by government rule and regulation. Sometimes their voices are louder than ours, but they are not yet a majority.

An example of that vocal superiority is evident in a controversy now going on in Washington. And since I'm involved, I've been waiting to hear from the parents of young America. How far are they willing to go in giving to government their prerogatives as parents?

Let me state the case as briefly and simply as I can. An organization of citizens, sincerely motivated and deeply concerned about the increase of illegitimate births and abortions involving girls well below the age of consent, sometime ago established a nationwide network of clinics to offer help to these girls, and, hopefully alleviate this situation. Now, again, let me say, I do not fault their intent. However, in their well-intentioned effort, these clinics have decided to provide advice and birth control drugs and devices to underage girls without the knowledge of their parents.

For some years now, the Federal Government has helped with funds to subsidize these clinics. In providing for this, the Congress decreed that every effort would be made to maximize parental participation. Nevertheless, the drugs and devices are prescribed without getting parental consent or giving notification after they've done so. Girls termed "sexually active"—and that has replaced the word "promiscuous"—are given this help in order to prevent illegitimate birth or abortions.

Well, we have ordered clinics receiving Federal funds to notify the parents such help has been given. One of the Nation's leading newspapers has created the term "squeal rule" in editorializing against us for doing this, and we're being criticized for violating the privacy of young people. A judge has recently granted an injunction against an enforcement of our rule. I've watched TV panel shows discuss this issue, seen columnists pontificating on our error, but no one seems to mention morality as playing a part in the subject of sex.

Is all of Judeo-Christian tradition wrong? Are we to believe that something so sacred can be looked upon as a purely physical thing with no potential for emotional and psychological harm? And isn't it the parents' right to give counsel and advice to keep their children from making mistakes that may affect their entire lives?

Many of us in government would like to know what parents think about this intrusion in their family by government. We're going to fight in the courts. The right of parents and the rights of family take precedence over those to Washington-based bureaucrats and social engineers.

But the fight against parental notification is really only one example of many attempts to water down traditional values and even abrogate the original terms of American democracy. Freedom prospers when religion is vibrant and the rule of law under

God is acknowledged. When our Founding Fathers passed the first amendment, they sought to protect churches from government interference. They never intended to construct a wall of hostility between government and the concept of religious belief itself.

The evidence of this permeates our history and our government. The Declaration of Independence mentions the Supreme Being no less than four times. "In God We Trust" is engraved on our coinage. The Supreme Court opens its proceedings with a religious invocation. And the Members of Congress open their sessions with a prayer. I just happen to believe the school children of the United States are entitled to the same privileges as Supreme Court Justices and Congressmen.

Last year, I sent the Congress a constitutional amendment to restore prayer to public schools. Already this session, there's growing bipartisan support for the amendment, and I am calling on the Congress to act speedily to pass it and to let our children pray.

Perhaps some of you read recently about the Lubbock school case, where a judge actually ruled that it was unconstitutional for a school district to give equal treatment to religious and non-religious student groups even when the group meetings were being held during the students' own time. The first amendment never intended to require government to discriminate against religious speech.

Senators Denton and Hatfield have proposed legislation in the Congress on the whole question of prohibiting discrimination against religious forms of student speech. Such legislation could go far to restore freedom of religious speech for public school students. And I hope the Congress considers these bills quickly. And with your help, I think it's possible we could also get the constitutional amendment through the Congress this year.

More than a decade ago, a Supreme Court decision literally wiped off the books of 50 States statutes protecting the rights of unborn children. Abortion on demand now takes the lives of up to 1 1/2 million unborn children a year. Human life legislation ending this tragedy will some day pass the Congress, and you and I must never rest until it does. Unless and until it can be proven that the unborn child is not a living entity, then its right to life, liberty, and the pursuit of happiness must be protected.

You may remember that when abortion on demand began, many, and, indeed, I'm sure many of you, warned that the practice would lead to a decline in respect for human life, that the philosophical premises used to justify abortion on demand would ultimately be used to justify other attacks on the sacredness of human life—infanticide or mercy killing. Tragically enough, those warnings proved all too true. Only last year a court permitted the death by starvation of a handicapped infant.

I have directed the Health and Human Services Department to make clear to every health care facility in the United States that the Rehabilitation Act of 1973 protects all handicapped persons against discrimination based on handicaps, including infants. And we have taken the further step of requiring that each and every recipient of Federal funds who provides health care services to infants must post and keep posted in a conspicuous place a notice stating that "discriminatory failure to feed and care for handicapped infants in this facility is prohibited by Federal law." It also lists a 24-hour, toll-free number so that nurses and others may report violations in time to save the infant's life.

In addition, recent legislation introduced in the Congress by Representative Henry Hyde of Illinois not only increases restrictions on publicly financed abortions, it also addresses this whole problem of infanticide. I urge the Congress to begin hearings and to adopt legislation that will protect the right of life of all children, including the disabled or handicapped.

Now, I'm sure that you must get discouraged at times, but you've done better than you know, perhaps. There's a great spiritual awakening in America, a renewal of the traditional values that have been the bedrock of America's goodness and greatness.

One recent survey by a Washington-based research council

concluded that Americans were far more religious than the people of other nations; 95 percent of those surveyed expressed a belief in God and a huge majority believed the Ten Commandments had real meaning in their lives. And another study has found that an overwhelming majority of Americans disapprove of adultery, teenage sex, pornography, abortion, and hard drugs. And this same study showed a deep reverence for the importance of family ties and religious belief.

I think the items that we've discussed here today must be a key part of the Nation's political agenda. For the first time the Congress is openly and seriously debating and dealing with the prayer and abortion issues—and that's enormous progress right there. I repeat: America is in the midst of a spiritual awakening and a moral renewal. And with your Biblical keynote, I say today, "Yes, let justice roll on like a river, righteousness like a never-failing stream."

Now, obviously, much of this new political and social consensus I've talked about is based on a positive view of American history, one that takes pride in our country's accomplishments and record. But we must never forget that no government schemes are going to perfect man. We know that living in this world means dealing with what philosophers would call the phenomenology of evil or, as theologians would put it, the doctrine of sin.

There is sin and evil in the world, and we're enjoined by Scripture and the Lord Jesus to oppose it with all our might. Our nation, too, has a legacy of evil with which it must deal. The glory of this land has been its capacity for transcending the moral evils of our past. For example, the long struggle of minority citizens for equal rights, once a source of disunity and civil war, is now a point of pride for all Americans. We must never go back. There is no room for racism, anti-Semitism, or other forms of ethnic and racial hatred in this country.

I know that you've been horrified, as have I, by the resurgence of some hate groups preaching bigotry and prejudice. Use the mighty voice of your pulpits and the powerful standing of your churches to denounce and isolate these hate groups in our midst. The commandment given us is clear and simple: "Thou shalt love thy neighbor as thyself."

But whatever sad episodes exist in our past, any objective observer must hold a positive view of American history, a history that has been the story of hopes fulfilled and dreams made into reality. Especially in this country, American has kept alight the torch of freedom, but not just for ourselves but for millions of others around the world.

And this brings me to my final point today. During my first press conference as President, in answer to a direct question, I pointed out that, as good Marxist-Leninists, the Soviet leaders have openly and publicly declared that the only morality they recognize is that which will further their cause, which is world revolution. I think I should point out I was only quoting Lenin, their guiding spirit, who said in 1920 that they repudiate all morality that proceeds from supernatural ideas—that's their name for religion—or ideas that are outside class conceptions. Morality is entirely subordinate to the interests of class war. And everything is moral that is necessary for the annihilation of the old, exploiting social order and for uniting the proletariat.

Well, I think the refusal of many influential people to accept this elementary fact of Soviet doctrine illustrates an historical reluctance to see totalitarian powers for what they are. We saw this phenomenon in the 1930s. We see it too often today.

This doesn't mean we should isolate ourselves and refuse to seek an understanding with them. I intend to do everything I can to persuade them of our peaceful intentions, to remind them that it was the West that refused to use this nuclear monopoly in the forties and fifties for territorial gain and which now proposes 50-percent cut in strategic ballistic missiles and an entire class of land-based, intermediate-range nuclear missiles.

At the same time, however, they must be made to understand we will never compromise our principles and standards. We will never give away our freedom. We will never abandon our belief in God. And we will never stop searching for a genuine peace. But we can assure none of these things America stands for through the so-called nuclear freeze solutions proposed by some.

The truth is that a freeze now would be a very dangerous fraud, for that is merely the illusion of peace. The reality is that we must find peace through strength.

I would agree to a freeze if only we could freeze the Soviet's global desires. A freeze at current levels of weapons would remove any incentive for the Soviets to negotiate seriously in Geneva and virtually end our chances to achieve the major arms reductions which we have proposed. Instead, they would achieve their objectives through the freeze.

A freeze would reward the Soviet Union for its enormous and unparalleled military buildup. It would prevent the essential and long overdue modernization of United States and allied defenses and would leave our aging forces increasingly vulnerable. And an honest freeze would require extensive prior negotiations on the systems and numbers to be limited and on the measures to ensure effective verification and compliance. And the kind of freeze that has been suggested would be virtually impossible to verify. Such a major effort would divert us completely from our current negotiations on achieving substantial reductions.

A number of years ago, I heard a young father, a very prominent young man in the entertainment world, addressing a tremendous gathering in California. It was during the time of the cold war, and communism and our own way of life were very much on people's minds. And he was speaking to that subject. And suddenly, though, I heard him saying, "I love my little girls more than anything—" And I said to myself, "Oh, no don't. You can't—don't say that." But I had underestimated him. He went on: "I would rather see my little girls die now, still believing in God, than have them grow up under communism and one day die no longer believing in God."

There were thousands of young people in that audience. They came to their feet with shouts of joy. They had instantly recognized the profound truth in what he had said, with regard to the physical and the soul and what was truly important.

Yes, let us pray for the salvation of all of those who live in that totalitarian darkness—pray they will discover the joy of knowing God. But until they do, let us be aware that while they preach the supremacy of the state, declare its omnipotence over individual man, and predict its eventual domination of all people on the Earth, they are the focus of evil in the modern world.

It was C. S. Lewis who, in his unforgettable "Screwtape Letters," wrote: "The greatest evil is not done now in those sordid 'dens of crime' that Dickens loved to paint. It is not even done in concentration camps and labor camps. In those we see its final result. But it is conceived and ordered (moved, seconded, carried and minuted) in clear, carpeted, warmed, and well-lighted offices, by quiet men with white collars and cut fingernails and smooth-shaven cheeks who do not need to raise their voice."

Well, because these "quiet men" do not "raise their voices," because they sometimes speak in soothing tones of brotherhood and peace, because, like other dictators before them, they're always making "their final territorial demand," some would have us accept them at their word and accommodate ourselves to their aggressive impuses. But if history teaches anything, it teaches that simple-minded appeasement or wishful thinking about our adversaries is folly. It means the betrayal of our past, the squandering of our freedom.

So, I urge you to speak out against those who would place the United States in a position of military and moral inferiority. You know, I've always believed that old Screwtape reserved his best efforts for those of you in the church. So, in your discussions of the nuclear freeze proposals, I urge you to beware the temptation of pride—the temptation of blithely declaring yourselves above it all and label both sides equally at fault, to ignore the facts of history and the aggressive impulses of an evil empire, to simply call the arms race a giant misunderstanding and thereby remove yourself from the struggle between right and wrong and good and evil.

I ask you to resist the attempts of those who would have you withhold your support for our efforts, this administration's efforts, to keep America strong and free, while we negotiate real and verifiable reductions in the world's nuclear arsenals and one day, with God's help, their total elimination.

While America's military strength is important, let me add here that I've always maintained that the struggle now going on for the world will never be decided by bombs or rockets, by armies or military might. The real crisis we face today is a spiritual one; at root, it is a test of moral will and faith.

Whittaker Chambers, the man whose own religious conversion made him a witness to one of the terrible traumas of our time, the Hiss-Chambers case, wrote that the crisis of the Western World exists to the degree in which the West is indifferent to God, the degree to which it collaborates in communism's attempt to make man stand alone without God. And then he said, for Marxism-Leninism is actually the second oldest faith, first proclaimed in the Garden of Eden with the words of temptation, "Ye shall be as gods."

The Western World can answer this challenge, he wrote, "but only provided that its faith in God and the freedom He enjoins is as great as Communism's faith in Man."

I believe we shall rise to the challenge. I believe that communism is another sad, bizarre chapter in human history whose last pages even now are being written. I believe this because the source of our strength in the quest for human freedom is not material, but spiritual. And because it knows no limitation, it must terrify and ultimately triumph over those who would enslave their fellow man. For the words of Isaiah: "He giveth power to the faint; and to them that have no might He increased

Yes, change your world. One of our Founding Fathers, Thomas Paine, said, "We have it within our power to begin the world over again." We can do it, doing together what no one church could do by itself.

God bless you, and thank you very much.

"Unknown Serviceman of the Vietnam Conflict," May 5, 1984

An American hero has returned home. God bless him.

We may not know of this man's life, but we know of his character. We may not know his name, but we know his courage. He is the heart, the spirit, and the soul of America.

Today, a grateful nation mourns the death of an unknown serviceman of the Vietnam conflict. This young American understood that freedom is never more than one generation away from extinction. He may not have wanted to be a hero, but there was a need—in the Iron Triangle, off Yankee Station, at Khe Sanh, over the Red River Valley.

He accepted his mission and did his duty. And his honest patriotism overwhelms us. We understand the meaning of his sacrifice and those of his comrades yet to return.

This American hero may not need us, but surely we need him. In Longfellow's words:

So when a great man dies,
For years beyond our ken,
The light he leaves behind him lies
Upon the paths of men.

We must not be blind to the light that he left behind. Our path must be worthy of his trust. And we must not betray his love of country. It's up to us to protect the proud heritage now in our hands, and to live in peace as bravely as he died in war.

On this day, as we honor our unknown serviceman, we pray to Almighty God for His mercy. And we pray for the wisdom that this hero may be America's last unknown.

166

BIBLIOGRAPHY

I. Primary Sources

Reagan, Ronald Wilson. *Along Wit's Trail: The Humor and Wisdom of Ronald Reagan*, edited by L. William Troxler. New York: Holt, Rinehart and Winston, 1984.
——— . *A Time for Choosing: The Speeches of Ronald Reagan, 1961–1982*, edited by Alfred Balitzer. Chicago: Regnery Gateway, 1983.
———. *The Creative Society: Some Comments on Some Problems Facing America.* New York: Devin-Adair, 1968.
Weekly Compilation of Presidential Documents. Washington. D.C.: Office of the Federal Register, National Archives and Records Service, General Services Administration.

II. On Reagan

A. BOOKS

Ackerman, Frank. *Reaganomics: Rhetoric vs. Reality.* Boston: South End Press, 1982.
Boyarsky, Bill. *Ronald Reagan, His Life and Rise to the Presidency.* New York: Random House, 1981.

Bibliography

Cannon, Lou. *Reagan.* New York: G. P. Putnam and Sons, 1982.

Dallek, Robert. *Ronald Reagan: The Politics of Symbolism.* Cambridge: Harvard University Press, 1984.

DeMausse, Lloyd. *Reagan's America.* New York: Creative Roots, 1984.

Dugger, Ronnie. *On Reagan: The Man and His Presidency.* New York: McGraw-Hill, 1983.

Evans, Rowland and Robert Novak. *The Reagan Revolution.* New York: Dutton, 1981.

Green, Mark and MacColl, Gail, editors. *There He Goes Again: Ronald Reagan's Reign of Error.* New York: Pantheon Books, 1983.

Hart, Roderick P., "The Great Communicator and Beyond." *Verbal Style and the Presidency* (Orlando, Florida: Academic Press, 1984) pp. 212-237.

Hobbs, Charles D. *Ronald Reagan's Call to Action.* New York: Thomas Nelson, 1976.

McClelland, Doug. *Hollywood on Ronald Reagan.* Winchester, Massachusetts: Faber and Faber, 1983.

Palmer, John L. and Sawhill, Isabel V. *The Reagan Record: An Assessment of America's Changing Domestic Priorities (An Urban Institute Study).* Cambridge: Ballinger Publishing, 1984.

Reagan, Ronald. *Where's the Rest of Me?* New York: Duell, Sloan and Pearce, 1965.

B. ARTICLES

Farrell, Kathleen and Theodore Otto Windt, Jr. "Presidential Rhetoric and Presidential Power: The Reagan Initiatives," in *Essays in Presidential Rhetoric,* edited by Theodore Windt and Beth Ingold. Dubuque: Kendall/Hunt, 1983, pp. 310-322.

Hart, Roderick P. "The Language of the Modern Presidency," *Presidential Studies Quarterly,* XIV, 2 (1984), pp. 265-288.

Ingold, Beth A. J. and Theodore Otto Windt, Jr. "Trying to 'Stay the Course': President Reagan's Rhetoric During the 1982 Election," *Presidential Studies Quarterly,* XIV, 14 (1984), pp. 87-97.

Rowland, Robert C. and Roger A. Payne. "The Context-Embeddedness of Political Discourse: A Re-Evaluation of Reagan's Rhetoric in the 1982 Midterm Election Campaign," *Presidential Studies Quarterly,* XIV, 4 (1984), pp. 486-499.

III. General Studies

A. BOOKS

Andrews, James R. *The Practice of Rhetorical Criticism.* New York: Macmillan, 1983.

Bercovitch, Sacvan. *The American Jeremiad*. Madison: The University of Wisconsin Press, 1978.

———. *The Puritan Origins of the American Self*. New Haven: Yale University Press, 1975.

Boorstin, Daniel. *The Image, or What Happened to the American Dream*. New York: Athenum, 1962.

Barber, James D. *The Presidential Character: Predicting Performance in the White House*. Englewood Cliffs, New Jersey: Prentice-Hall, 1977.

Burke, Kenneth. *A Grammar of Motives*. Berkeley: University of California Press, 1968.

———. *A Rhetoric of Motives*. Englewood Cliff, N.J. Prentice-Hall, 1950.

———. *Language as Symbolic Action: Essays on Life, Literature, and Method*. Berkeley: University of California Press, 1966.

Corbett, Edward P. J. *Classical Rhetoric for the Modern Student*. New York Oxford University Press, 1971.

Cuthberston, G. M. *Political Myth and Epic*. East Lansing: Michigan State University Press, 1975.

Edelman, Murray. *Political Language: Words that Succeed and Policies that Fail*. New York: Academic Press, 1977.

Ellul, Jacques. *The Political Illusion*, translated by K. Kellen. New York: Knopf, 1967.

Hart, Roderick P. *The Political Pulpit*. West Lafayette, Indiana: Purdue University Press, 1977.

Hofstadter, Richard. *"The Paranoid Style in American Politics" and Other Essays*. New York: Vintage Books, 1964.

Neustadt, Richard E. *Presidential Power: The Politics of Leadership*. New York: Wiley, 1976.

Nichols, Marjorie Hochmuth. *Rhetoric and Criticism*. Baton Rouge: Louisiana State University Press, 1967.

Novak, Michael. *Choosing Our King: Powerful Symbols in Positive Politics*. New York: Macmillan, 1974.

Jones, Donald G. and Russel E. Richey, editors. *American Civil Religion*. New York: Harper and Row, 1974.

Rueckert, W., editor. *Critical Responses to Kenneth Burke*. Minneapolis: University of Minnesota Press, 1966.

Sennett, Richard. *The Fall of Public Man*. New York: Knopf, 1977.

Tudor, Henry. *Political Myth*. New York: Praeger, 1973.

B. ARTICLES

Bennett, W. Lance. "The Ritualistic and Pragmatic Bases of Political Campaign Discourse," *Quarterly Journal of Speech*, 63 (October 1977), pp. 219–238.

Blankenship, Jane, Marlene G. Fine and Leslie K. Davis. "The 1980 Re-

Bibliography

publican Primary Debates: The Transformation of Actor to Scene," *Quarterly Journal of Speech*, 69 (1983), pp. 25–36.

Fairlie, Henry. "The Decline of Oratory," *The New Republic*, May 28, 1984, pp. 15–19.

Farrell, Thomas. "Knowledge, Consensus, and Rhetorical Theory," *Quarterly Journal of Speech*, 62 (1976), pp. 1–14.

Fisher, Walter. "Reaffirmation and Subversion of the American Dream," *Quarterly Journal of Speech*, 59 (1973), pp. 160–167.

———. "Rhetorical Fiction and the Presidency," *Quarterly Journal of Speech*, 66 (April, 1982), pp. 1–8.

Gold, Ellen R. "Political Apologia: The Ritual of Self-Defense," *Communication Monographs*, 45 (1975), pp. 306–316.

Gronbeck, Bruce. "The Functions of Presidential Campaigning," *Communication Monographs*, 45 (1978) pp. 268–280.

King, Andrew. "The Rhetoric of Power Maintainance; Elites at the Precipice," *Quarterly Journal of Speech*, (1976), pp. 127–134.

McBath, James and Walter Fisher. "Persuasion in Presidential Campaign Communication," *Quarterly Journal of Speech*, 55 (February, 1969), pp. 17–25.

McDonald, Lee. "Myth, Politics, and Political Science," *Western Political Quarterly*, 22 (1969), pp. 147–150.

Patton, John H. "A Government as Good as its People: Jimmy Carter and the Restoration of Transcendence to Politics," *Quarterly Journal of Speech*, 63 (October 1977), pp. 249–257.

Safire, William. "Ringing Rhetoric; The Return of Political Oratory" *The New York Times Magazine*, August 19, 1984, pp. 22ff.

Stelzner, Harmann. "The Quest Story and Nixon's November 3, 1969 Address," *Quarterly Journal of Speech*, 57 (April 1971), pp. 163–172.

Swanson, David. "The New Politics Meets the Old Rhetoric: New Directions in Campaign Communications Research," *Quarterly Journal of Speech*, 58 (February 1972), pp. 31–40.

Valley, David. "Significant Characteristics of Democratic Presidential Nomination Acceptance Speeches," *Central States Speech Journal*, 25 (1974), pp. 56–62.

INDEX

Index

Reagan, Nelle, 54
Reagan, Ronald, *life*: leads strike at
Eureka College, 13; works at
WHO, 14 ff.; goes to Hollywood,
15; fears being a "semi-automaton,"
15, 16; joins Screen Actors Guild,
16; testifies before House Un-
American Affairs Committee, 18;
works for General Electric, 18;
leaves General Electric, 22–23;
shift to conservative politics, 18–21;
becomes Republican, 24; childhood, 52–53; religious views,
73–74; *speeches*: American Bar Association, 1983, 2; Departure from
Los Angeles, 1981, 5; "A Time for
Choosing," 1964, 12, 25–30,
124–138; "Encroaching Control,"
1961, 22–23; Building and Con-
structions Trades Department of
AFL-CIO, 1981, 32–33; Corn
Growers Association, 1982, 34;
White House prayer breakfast,
1982, 36–37; "Government and the
Family," 1976, 37; *U.S.S. Constellation*, 1981, 38; Notre Dame
commencement, 1981, 38–49,
145–155; "Unknown Serviceman of
the Vietnam Conflict," 1984,
55–60, 166; Mother's Day, 1983,
54; Mother's Day, 1984, 54; Memorial Day, 1984, 55; Inauguration,
1981, 60–61, 67, 139–145; Joint
Session of Congress, 1981, 61; "The
Morality Gap at Berkeley," 1966,
62–63; "The Value of Understanding the Past" (Eureka library
dedication), 1967, 64; "Ours is Not
a Sick Society," 1970, 64; "Why the
Conservative Movement is Growing," 1973, 64–65; International
Association of Chiefs of Police,
1981, 67; New Year's Remarks to

Foreign Peoples, 1982, 68; "Reshaping the American Political
Landscape," 1977, 68, 73; Captive
Nations Week, 1982, 69; Charlottenburg Palace of Berlin, 1982,
69–71; American National Day of
Prayer, 1981, 73; National Religious Broadcasters, 1982, 74;
National Day of Prayer, 1982, 74;
Jesse Helms Dinner, 1983, 74;
State of the Union, 1984, 96–97;
National Association of Evangelicals in Orlando, 1983, 76–80,
155–166; Christmas Eve, 1981, 76;
Rosh Hashanah, 1982, 75; Conservative Political Action Conference,
1981, 81, 91; Medal of Freedom
ceremony, 1984, 81; Conservative
Political Action Conference, 1982,
82; West Point commencement,
1981, 89–90; Alf Landon's birthday,
1983, 90; Reagan's seventy-third
birthday celebration in Dixon,
1984, 91; Spirit of America Rally,
1984, 92; Nomination-acceptance
address, 1984, 93, 107; Atlanta,
1984, 100, 120, Election eve, 1984,
102; Olympic games opening day,
1984, 105; Post-Olympics breakfast,
1984, 106; Jefferson Junior High
School, 1984, 108, Detroit, 1984,
108; Charlotte, North Carolina,
1984, 108; Sedalia, Missouri, 1984,
109; Elizabeth, New Jersey, 1984,
120
Rockne, Knute, 39 ff.
Rosenblatt, Roger, 14

Speechwriting, 8, 10–11*n*10

Vietnam Memorial, 56

Winthrop, John, 2, 87–89

172